HURRICANE

OSPREY
PUBLISHING

CONTENTS

INTRODUCTION

Neither the prettiest nor highest performing fighter of World War II, the Hawker Hurricane should nonetheless rightfully be seen as the key to the Royal Air Force's victory in the Battle of Britain.

Its design incorporated older, tried and tested technologies, but married them to the latest in aeroengine design and the newfangled eight-gun armament, creating a fighter good enough to carry Great Britain successfully through its darkest hour.

Ironically, it was only through Hawker's foresight and persistence that the Hurricane was available in sufficient numbers to equip an expanding RAF Fighter Command at the outbreak of World War II. When George Bulman first took the prototype Hurricane into the air at Brooklands on 6 November 1935, it was presented to the world as a modern fighting monoplane.

OPPOSITE Hawker Hurricanes from No. 111 Squadron based at Northolt, in flight. (Photo by Popperfoto/Getty Images)

Impressed by its eight machine guns, retractable undercarriage and ability to breach 300mph with ease, many journalists of the day commented that the peak of fighter performance had finally been reached.

Yet the Air Ministry, responsible for procuring the UK's military aircraft, remained unconvinced, even as the dark clouds of another world conflict gathered. But with a rather more solid grip on the realities of the day, the Hawker Aircraft Company began production without a firm contract and the RAF received the aircraft it so urgently needed.

With No. 111 Squadron leading the way, only a handful of units were operational on the Hurricane at the outbreak of war. Thanks to sudden massive orders and well-organised manufacturing that subcontracted production to the Gloster Aircraft Company and General Aircraft, more squadrons were rapidly re-equipped, cutting their teeth during the Battle of France. But it was during the Battle of Britain that the Hurricane excelled, as Fighter Command's rugged backbone.

With technology advancing at high speed, the Supermarine Spitfire quickly overtook the Hurricane in the air-to-air role, although the Hawker remained the fighter of choice in North Africa and the Far East, where it often fought Japanese formations against overwhelming odds.

Many Hurricanes were shot down or badly damaged in action, only to rejoin the fray after hasty repairs, where more fragile designs would have been written off. A real workhorse in all respects, the Hurricane was also adapted for and excelled in the ground-attack role, carrying bombs, large-calibre cannon, rockets and drop tanks. It also provided sterling service with the Royal Navy's Fleet Air Arm, flying off catapult-armed ships and aircraft carriers in some of the war's fiercest weather.

Many Hurricanes were relegated to second line units during the later stages of World War II, although the type fought on in the Far East, especially Burma, wreaking havoc upon enemy ground units. The last of the RAF's frontline Hurricanes served with No. 6 Squadron in Palestine until 1947, but two of the type remain on Royal Air Force strength with the Battle of Britain Memorial Flight at RAF Coningsby, Lincolnshire.

The ranks of airworthy Hurricanes have swelled in recent years, with Hurricanes and Sea Hurricanes flying in the UK and overseas. There is also no shortage of airframes on museum display, these survivors remaining as a lasting memory of one of the most significant fighter aircraft in world history and perhaps the most important in the annals of the RAF and the British nation.

OPPOSITE Two Hurricanes and a Spitfire from the Battle of Britain Memorial Flight conduct a flypast over Horse Guards Parade in central London on May 10, 2015 to mark the 70th anniversary of VE Day. (BEN STANSALL/AFP/Getty Images)

CHRONOLOGY

1920
15 Nov   H. G. Hawker Engineering established.

1928
August   Hawker F.20/27 biplane fighter prototype flies for the first time.

1929
March   Hornet biplane fighter prototype flies for the first time.

1931
25 March   Fury I biplane fighter flies for the first time.

1933
August   Hawker Chief Designer Sydney Camm discusses future RAF fighter requirements with Air Ministry's Directorate of Technical Development.

1934
15 June   PV.3 biplane fighter demonstrator flies for the first time.
August   Hawker design shown to Air Ministry, which issues Specification F.36/34 for a monoplane fighter based on the company's project.
September   Hawker's Interceptor Monoplane now becomes the Air Ministry's F.36/34 Single-Seat Fighter – High-Speed Monoplane, powered by the Rolls-Royce PV.12.

OPPOSITE A Hurricane IIC of No. 87 Squadron, 1942. (Photo by Charles E. Brown/Royal Air Force Museum/Getty Images)

1935

18 February   Prototype F.36/34 Single-Seat Fighter – High Speed Monoplane ordered.

6 November   Hurricane prototype K5083 completes its first flight at Brooklands. Three more flights follow that month.

1936

18 Feb   Official Hurricane trials begin at Martlesham Heath.

5 March   Supermarine Type 300, later named Spitfire, makes its first flight.

23 April   Hurricane proposal armed with four 20mm Oerlikon cannon tendered against F.37/35.

3 June   Air Ministry orders 600 F.36/34 Single-Seat Fighters.

27 June   Air Ministry accepts the name 'Hurricane' for the new Hawker fighter.

3 Dec   First flight of a production Fury II biplane fighter.

1937

12 Oct   First flight of production Hurricane I.

15 Dec   First Hurricane Is reach the front line, equipping No. 111 Sqn at RAF Northolt.

1938

10 Feb   Sqn Ldr J. W. Gillan, commanding No. 111 Sqn, flies from Turnhouse, near Edinburgh, to Northolt in 48 minutes at an average speed of 408.75mph.

March   No. 3 Squadron begins receiving Hurricanes at Kenley.

May   No. 56 Squadron begins receiving Hurricanes at North Weald.

July   No. 87 Squadron begins receiving Hurricanes at Debden.

No. 73 Squadron begins receiving Hurricanes at Digby.

September   No. 85 Squadron begins receiving Hurricanes at Debden.

	No. 32 Squadron begins receiving Hurricanes at Biggin Hill.
October	No. 1 Squadron begins receiving Hurricanes at Tangmere.
November	Nos. 43 and 79 Squadrons begin receiving Hurricanes at Tangmere.

1939

January	No. 213 Squadron begins receiving Hurricanes at Wittering.
February	No. 46 Squadron begins receiving Hurricanes at Digby.
March	No. 501 (County of Gloucester) Squadron begins receiving Hurricanes at Filton.
2 March	A pattern Hurricane is sent to Canada to inform Canadian production.
May	No. 504 (County of Nottingham) Squadron begins receiving Hurricanes at Hucknall.
September	Outbreak of World War II: by this time,

	18 RAF squadrons are equipped with the Hurricane.
27 Oct	First Gloster-built Hurricane I makes its maiden flight.
30 Oct	A Hurricane I of No. 1 Sqn is the first RAF aircraft to destroy a German aircraft over the Western Front in World War II.
2 Nov	A No. 73 Squadron Hurricane I shoots down an enemy aircraft over France.
21 Nov	A No. 85 Squadron Hurricane I shoots down an He 111 off Boulogne.
23 Nov	Hurricane Is of No. 1 Sqn shoot down a Heinkel He 111.
30 Nov	The Winter War between Finland and the Soviet Union begins.

1940

February	12 Hurricanes shipped to Finland.
13 March	The Winter War ends.
26 March	First clash between the Hurricane and Messerschmitt Bf 110, with Hurricane Is

of No. 73 Sqn in combat with Bf 110Cs of 13.(Z)/LG 1.

Flg Off Edgar James 'Cobber' Kain becomes the first Hurricane ace, shooting down two Bf 109s to bring his score to five.

10 May No. 46 Squadron embarks in HMS *Glorious*, bound for Norway.

German army begins its push west through the Netherlands, Belgium, and Luxembourg towards France.

11 May No. 87 Squadron shoots down ten Ju 87s for the loss of two pilots and their Hurricanes.

12 May No. 3 Squadron shoots down eight enemy aircraft without loss.

20 May Kent-based Hurricane squadrons instructed to attack German columns on the Cambrai–Arras road in preparation for Operation *Dynamo*.

22 May No. 85 Squadron withdraws from France.

24 May No. 87 Squadron withdraws from France.

25 May No. 46 Squadron Hurricanes take off from HMS *Glorious* for Skånland and Bardufoss.

26 May Operation *Dynamo*, the evacuation of Allied troops from Dunkirk, begins.

28 May 46 Squadron Hurricanes shoot down a Ju 88 and two Do 26s.

June By now, 386 Hurricane Is have been lost in the ill-fated defence of France.

3 June British withdrawal from Norway begins.

3/4 June The last of 328,226 British and French troops are evacuated from Dunkirk.

7/8 June All ten surviving 46 Squadron Hurricanes land back aboard HMS *Glorious*.

OPPOSITE Hurricane Mk IIs in flight. (Photo by Popperfoto/Getty Images)

8 June	German battlecruisers *Scharnhorst* and *Gneisenau* sink HMS *Glorious* at 1740hrs. Only 40 men survive, including No. 46 Squadron's CO and one other pilot. Nos. 17 and 242 Squadrons deploy to Le Mans.
11 June	The Hurricane Mk II prototype flies for the first time.
17 June	No. 73 Squadron leaves France via St Malo after burning its surviving Hurricanes at Nantes.
18 June	No. 1 Squadron is evacuated via St Nazaire.
19 June	No. 501 Squadron covers the evacuation of troops from Cherbourg.
20 June	No. 501 Squadron returns its eight surviving Hurricanes to Britain.

OPPOSITE A Hurricane Mk XIIA 5711 (G-HURI) fighter aircraft performs an aerobatic display at the IWM Duxford on October 18, 2012. (Photo by Oli Scarff/Getty Images)

July–October	Fighter Command deploys 1,715 Hurricane Is in the defence of Great Britain, and they are credited with destroying 1,593 German aircraft, four-fifths of all the enemy aircraft destroyed during the Battle of Britain.
7 July	Hurricanes of Nos. 145, 43 and 601 Squadrons shoot down three Dorniers.
10 July	At the beginning of the Battle of Britain, Fighter Command has 32 Hurricane I squadrons. In the Hurricane's largest dogfight yet, 22 Hurricanes from No. 32, 56 and 111 Squadrons, along with eight No. 74 Squadron Spitfires, engage 26 Do 17 and Do 215 bombers, 30 Bf 110s and 20 Bf 109Es.
2 August	418 Flight takes off from HMS *Argus* to deliver Hurricanes to Malta.
16 August	No. 249 Squadron Hurricane pilot Flt Lt E. J. B. Nicolson flies a relentless attack

on a Bf 110 despite his own serious injuries. The action was subsequently recognised with Fighter Command's first and only Victoria Cross.

19 August	No. 274 Squadron re-forms at Amiriya, becoming the first all-Hurricane unit in the Middle East.
31 August	The Battle of Britain Hurricane units suffer their worst mauling yet, as Nos. 56 and 79 Squadrons each lose four; 1 (RCAF) and 601 Squadrons three apiece; 85, 151, 253, 257 and 310 Squadrons each lose two; and 1, 111, and 501 Squadrons suffer individual losses.
28 October	Italy invades Greece.
November	605 (County of Warwick) Squadron is the first unit to receive Hurricane Mk IIs.
11 Nov	Nos. 17, 46 and 257 Squadrons intercept a force of ten Italian BR.20 bombers escorted by 40 CR.42s, G.50s and a few Bf 109Es, bound for Harwich. Nine enemy aircraft are shot down.

1941

9 January	Malta-based No. 261 Squadron shoots down four Macchi MC.200 fighter-bombers.
February	No. 56 Squadron is the first unit to receive the Hurricane Mk IIB.
20 February	No. 80 Squadron flies its first Hurricane operation in Greece.
28 February	Flg Off Richard 'Ape' Cullen shoots down two SM.79s and two CR.42s, and shares a BR.20 in a single combat over Albania, earning him the DFC.
March	Sea Hurricane Mk IB flies for the first time.
April	No. 3 Squadron is the first unit to receive the Hurricane Mk IIC.
20 April	Sqn Ldr 'Pat' Pattle, the highest-scoring Hurricane ace, is shot down and killed in combat with Bf 110s.

2 August	Lt Cdr R. W. H. Everett launches from HMS *Maplin* to score the Sea Hurricane's first kill.
September	The prototype Hurricane Mk IID flies for the first time.
7 September	Nos. 81 and 134 Squadrons arrive with their Hurricane Mk IIBs at Vaenga, Russia, in HMS *Argus*.

1942

13 January	Nos. 17, 135, 136 and 232 Squadron pilots arrive at Seletar, Singapore, flying Hurricane Mk IIBs as No. 232 Squadron.
15 February	Nos. 232 and 258 Squadrons withdraw with the fall of Singapore.
6 June	No. 6 Squadron takes the Hurricane Mk IID into action for the first time.
19 August	Nos. 3, 43, 87 and 245 Squadrons all fly the Hurricane Mk II during the Dieppe raid.

1943

| July | No. 6 Squadron is the first unit to receive the Hurricane Mk IV. |
| 29 July | No. 184 Squadron is the first unit to successfully attack shipping with rockets. |

1944

| February | No. 67 Squadron replaces its Hurricane Mk IICs with the Spitfire Mk VIII. |
| May | No. 135 Squadron replaces its Hurricanes as it becomes the first RAF unit to receive the Republic Thunderbolt. |

1945

| 15 June | No. 351 Squadron transfers to the Yugoslav Air Force. |

1946

| February | No. 6 Squadron withdraws the Hurricane Mk IV. Its aircraft are the last frontline Hurricanes in RAF service. |

DESIGN AND DEVELOPMENT

The Sopwith Aviation Company's scouts (fighter aircraft) made a great contribution to the Allied effort during World War I, its excellent designs including the Tabloid, 1½-Strutter, Pup, Triplane and, of course, the iconic Camel. Tommy Sopwith was something of a visionary when it came to fighter design, his work including the Swallow, a monoplane version of the Camel, although its performance did not warrant further development.

The massive surplus of military aircraft following the Armistice helped put paid to Sopwith's hopes for post-war success, and although it built ABC Motorcycles' machines under licence in an attempt to survive, a 1920 claim from the Treasury for Excess War Profits Duty sealed the company's fate. Undeterred,

OPPOSITE Hurricanes being assembled in the factory, 20 July 1938. (Photo by Keystone-France/Gamma-Rapho via Getty Images)

Tommy Sopwith, along with Harry Hawker and Fred Sigrist, his wartime partners, and engineers Bill Eyre and F. I. Bennett, immediately formed H. G. Hawker Engineering, building motorcycles of its own design, aluminium bodies for AC Cars, and aeroplanes.

Its flying base at the traditional home of British aviation, Brooklands, proved particularly advantageous, since Vickers Ltd, another aviation manufacturer, also called it home. Captain Thomson, Hawker's fledgling chief designer, created its first aircraft, the Duiker, with heavy reliance on equipment and parts loaned and manufactured, respectively, by Vickers.

Designed to meet a reconnaissance requirement, the Duiker made its first flight in July 1923. No orders were forthcoming, but Hawker learned a great deal and its next design progressed considerably further than a single prototype.

Ironically, the Duiker had not been Hawker's first design to fly. In 1922, the company responded to Specification 25/22, for a night fighter, with the Thomson-designed Woodcock. The first prototype, J6987, took its first flight, with F. P. Raynham at the controls, in March 1923. It was rejected, and W. G. Carter replaced Thomson as chief designer.

Carter redesigned the aircraft into the successful Woodcock II, of which the RAF eventually ordered 62. The design also gave the company its first overseas sales, the Danish government buying three examples of the Danecock version. The Danes subsequently built a dozen more aircraft under licence as the Dankok. Hawker was on its way.

Throughout the 1920s and into the early 1930s, Hawker achieved varying success with its fighters, and torpedo and light bombers, especially the Hart, which led to a family of derivatives that became an RAF mainstay from 1930 into World War II. In 1925, Sydney Camm became chief designer, having begun his aviation career as a carpenter's apprentice at Martinsyde, before progressing to Hawker in 1923 as a senior draughtsman.

The Hurricane's lineage began in the late 1920s with Air Ministry Specification F.20/27 for an 'interceptor single-seat fighter', against which manufacturers Armstrong Whitworth, Bristol, de Havilland, Fairey, Hawker, Saunders-Roe, Vickers and Westland all bid. Built only as a prototype, the Hawker F.20/27 first flew in August 1928 as a single-seat biplane powered by a 520hp Mercury radial. It was simultaneously being redesigned to accommodate a new V12 engine, the Rolls-Royce F.XI, later known as the Kestrel.

Named Hornet, this revised aircraft first flew from Brooklands in March 1929, powered by a 420hp F.XIC engine. Soon it was re-engined with a 480hp Kestrel IS and in early 1930 the Air Ministry purchased it for extended evaluation at Martlesham Heath. The Air Ministry placed an order for 21 aircraft in 1930, and the design was renamed Fury. The Fury I first flew from Brooklands on 25 March 1931, with Hawker chief test pilot George Bulman at the controls.

BREACHING THE 200MPH BARRIER

The Fury was an outstanding fighter and the first in RAF service to achieve 200mph. Prior to its service entry the RAF's fastest aircraft had been the Hawker Hart light bomber, the Fury therefore marking a vast improvement over contemporary fighters. It was also popular with pilots, and its responsive controls made it an excellent aerobatic mount.

Production Furies were fitted with the more powerful 525hp Kestrel, for a good climb rate of more than 2,400ft per minute and a top speed of 207mph at 14,000ft. In May 1931 this beautiful aircraft entered service with No. 43 Squadron at Tangmere, remaining in the front line until 1938.

In the meantime, another new specification, F.7/30, called for a fighter capable of no less than 250mph at 10,000ft, armed with four machine guns and capable of

RIGHT Hawker Fury Mk Is of No. 1 Squadron, in flight rehearsing for display at Zurich, Tangmere, 1937. (Photo by Charles E. Brown/Royal Air Force Museum/Getty Images)

operating by day or night. Since the Fury had already been ordered, it was effectively ruled out, but this did not stop Camm, unwisely in the eyes of many in the industry, from pursuing further development of his sleek fighter.

Many of the manufacturers who began development work misinterpreted the specification, including Blackburn, Bristol, Gloster, Supermarine and Westland. This, aggravated by the Air Ministry's preference for the liquid-cooled Kestrel IV (later Goshawk) engine, resulted in Britain's fighter development stalling during the early 1930s. Three main contenders emerged for Specification F.7/30, the Supermarine Type 224, Westland PV.4 and Blackburn F.3. None came close to the proposed 250mph top speed, and the F.3, which never flew, was only given an optimistic maximum speed of 190mph.

It was left to the Gloster Aircraft Company to design the RAF's next fighter, during the fading days of the F.7/30 specification in 1935, when it created a modified version of the Gauntlet, as the Gladiator. Hawker was already busy meeting orders for the Hart and its variations, including the Demon fighter, Audax army co-operation aircraft and Osprey general-purpose land and seaplane, as well as the Hardy, Hartebeest (or Hartbee), Hind and Hector, none of which stopped Camm proceeding with a fine-tuned version of the Fury as part of the F.7/30 competition.

First came the Intermediate Fury, however, built against F.7/30 requirements as a private venture for trials and registered G-ABSE. Various engines were fitted and its performance was encouraging. A new F.7/30 design then appeared as the PV.3, essentially an enlarged Fury powered by a 695hp steam-cooled Goshawk III engine; it first flew on 15 June 1934. Overheating problems were solved by incorporating steam condensers along the leading edge of the upper wing as well as a much smaller retractable radiator under the fuselage. Very little new ground was broken by the PV.3, which could still only manage 220mph, but many of its features were transferred onto the High Speed Fury that resulted in the operational Fury II. The RAF ordered 98 Fury IIs, the first entering service in 1936.

F.36/34 SINGLE-SEAT FIGHTER – HIGH SPEED MONOPLANE

Camm had been mulling over the concept of a 'Fury Monoplane' since 1933, and after sounding out several Air Ministry officials over the idea and receiving an encouraging response, he set to work, although elements in the Ministry remained reluctant to move away from the tried and tested biplane format.

Nonetheless, with new aircraft technologies becoming available, the Air Ministry issued specification F.5/34 in May 1934. It specified a monoplane fighter with an armament of six to eight guns and capable of at least 300mph. It was an almost exact match for the designs that Camm and Supermarine's chief designer, R. J. Mitchell, were already creating.

Previous British fighters had relied on the old 0.303in Vickers machine gun, which was prone to jamming, but a new initiative looked set to make the more reliable US-designed 0.3in Colt available, re-bored as the 0.303in Browning to match standard RAF ammunition. The Vickers had traditionally been positioned where a pilot could reach it to clear a jam, but the Browning's reliability meant it could be positioned in the wing.

Referring to its latest aircraft as 'Interceptor Monoplane to F.5/34', the Hawker design team at Canbury Park Road, Kingston set to work. Technical data was still lacking with regard to the Browning machine gun, so the aircraft was designed with a quartet of Vickers guns instead, two in the nose and one in each inner wing section. In the background, however, the team was investigating how best to accommodate eight machine guns in the outer wings, using Vickers gun dimensions.

By June 1934, a one-tenth scale model was ready for testing in the compressed air wind tunnel at the National Physics Laboratory, Teddington. Two months later, the test results proved the fighter's very satisfactory aerodynamic qualities up to 350mph. The trials were carried out under the assumption that a PV.12 engine would be fitted, giving an all up weight (auw) of 4,600lb. By now, Rolls-Royce confidently claimed that it could produce 1,000hp from the PV.12. During August 1934, Camm submitted the design, including potential performance figures and findings, to the Air Ministry.

Camm's design study must have been received with great enthusiasm, because within weeks a more detailed specification was written around his design. Hawker received F.6/34 in the last week of August, and by 4 September had formally tendered its design to the Air Ministry as the F.36/34 Single-Seat Fighter – High Speed Monoplane. Events now began unfolding at pace, motivated by Hawker and global events, since it increasingly looked as if another world war was looming.

ROLLS-ROYCE PV.12

On 17 November 1934, the first manufacturing drawings for the fuselage were issued to the experimental shops for jig preparation, but before the month was over a slight complication arose when Rolls-Royce informed Hawker that the PV.12's weight had increased by 80lb. This shifted the aircraft's centre of gravity, a vital parameter in its safe handling and aerodynamic performance, a change countered by increasing ammunition capacity by 400 rounds; auw increased to 4,800lb. More engine information was supplied on 18 December, when Rolls-Royce stated that the engine would produce a take-off rating power of 1,025hp at 2,900rpm.

A week later, Hawker received a PV.12 to install in a mock-up aircraft completed a couple of weeks earlier. The mock-up proved very useful in helping the designers and engineers with physical aspects of the cockpit layout, the pilot's field of vision, undercarriage retraction, cooling ducts, radiator position and gun mountings, which at this stage were still equipped for Vickers guns.

With the mock-up taking centre stage, a final conference was held at Canbury Park Road between Camm and the RAF's Air Commodore L. A. Pattinson, Air-Officer-

OPPOSITE A Gloster Gladiator I of No. 87 Squadron flying from RAF Debden, 1938. (Photo by Charles E. Brown/Royal Air Force Museum/Getty Images)

Commanding (AOC) Armament Group. The focus of these final discussions was the armament, which Camm was anxious to replace with a wing-mounted battery in the outer wings. Pattinson was well aware of the Vickers' poor performance, but stated that a satisfactory licence for the Browning was yet to be achieved. Air Ministry representatives had only recently returned from the US with licence terms, which were being studied by the Birmingham Small Arms Company (BSA).

Hawker was awarded Contract No. 357483/34 on 18 February 1935 for a single-fighter, to be registered K5083. A remarkable feature of this contract appeared under the appendix covering 'Standard of Preparation'. In this section, a statement read that 'no decision had yet been reached regarding the provision of armament'. It was agreed six weeks after the contract was issued that no armament should be fitted, but equivalent ballast employed to represent two fuselage-mounted Vickers and a Browning in each wing. At this stage no licence had been issued to produce the Browning but considering the decision to ballast for a pair of the weapons, it is puzzling as to why ballast for the full battery of eight was not ordered. Not until July 1935 was the situation resolved, BSA taking a licence to produce the Browning.

Construction of K5083 continued at Canbury Park Road, conveniently taking place below the design team's offices. Flight testing of the PV.12, which had by now been named Merlin, had begun in Hart K3036 on 21 February 1935. Progressive development revealed that a large radiator would be needed, but Hawker had other ideas. Rather than installing a high-drag unit, it was proposed that a duct fitted under the fuselage would speed up the airflow over a smaller radiator. The best way to achieve this was to ensure the air was not disrupted before it entered the duct. A very clean fuselage undersurface was therefore maintained and D-shaped doors fitted to cover the retracted main wheels.

OPPOSITE Prototype Hawker Hurricane being test flown by Hawker's Chief Test Pilot, Flight Lieutenant P. W. S. 'George' Bulman. It first took to the air on 6 November 1935. (Photo by The Print Collector/Print Collector/Getty Images)

K5083 was structurally complete by August 1935 and prepared for skinning, which would take another six weeks. Rolls-Royce Merlin C No. 11 was delivered and fitted around this time and with preliminary systems checks complete, the aircraft was prepared for a road move to Brooklands. On 23 October 1935, K5083, minus wings, was secured firmly under a tarpaulin and transported to the flight assembly shed at Brooklands. There the fabric-covered wings were refitted and the controls reconnected. The retractable undercarriage, which included the tailwheel, was tested, and the Merlin engine started.

FIRST FLIGHT

On 3 November 1935, George Bulman taxied the fighter onto the Brooklands grass, beginning the steady task of acclimatising himself to it. His first impressions centred on the improved visibility compared to a biplane, with 'more daylight in the cockpit', while he described the view as 'marvellous'. Bulman later told Camm he was particularly impressed with the ease of disembarkation.

A setback occurred on 4 November, when Rolls-Royce informed Hawker that the Merlin had failed to pass its 50-hour certification test. A quick inspection had failed to reveal why the engine lost power after just 40 hours. After consultation, Bulman suggested that the first flight go ahead providing there was no sign of a drop on the engine's magneto. Bulman also said the oil filter should be checked for metal fragments after every flight until Rolls-Royce had discovered the cause of the problem. The Hawker and Rolls-Royce engineers agreed with this cautious but positive approach.

On 6 November Bulman, with approximately 80 people watching, taxied K5083 out for its first flight. No press were informed, or invited, and photography was not permitted, such was the level of secrecy surrounding the aircraft. Taxiing to the end of the runway, the silver monoplane turned into wind and, with a roar from its Merlin, seemed to be into the air and over the banking of Brooklands' old motor racing circuit in no time at all.

Bulman was instantly impressed and content to carry out a general handling flight. He also performed a slow roll and reached 300mph in a gentle dive with ease; a stall test with undercarriage and flaps down revealed a stalling speed of 80mph, and quick recovery via slight forward pressure on the stick. After just over half an hour, Bulman floated back over the banking and, with its big Watts propeller seemingly hardly turning, the aircraft performed a gentle three-point landing. A jubilant Tommy Sopwith and Sydney Camm greeted him, after driving across the airfield in a Rolls-Royce.

Incredibly, Bulman never filed an official flight test report for this historic event, instead jotting down his impressions on a secretary's note pad. He briefed Camm, including comments about engine temperatures, which built up rapidly while taxiing. The temperature also increased quickly when the flaps were lowered, suggesting that the airflow was being retarded at the rear of the radiator. But his major complaint was about the aircraft's canopy, which constantly creaked and flexed in flight. His brief complete, Bulman gave Camm a broad grin, playfully punched him on the shoulder and said, 'Syd, you've most certainly got a winner here!'

A TROUBLESOME CHILD

The canopy was temporarily modified by the addition of an extra set of struts, but the overheating problems would only be resolved by redesigning the entire radiator fairing. The D-shaped undercarriage doors proved to be more trouble than they were worth and were removed. Initially, K5083 was fitted with a pair of tailplane struts, since tail flutter was anticipated in a dive. This never occurred and the struts were removed.

Bulman made five more flights in November and on 6 December a provisional airworthiness certificate was finally issued for the Merlin C engine. Yet the Merlin suffered a host of problems, including supercharger bearing failure, automatic boost control capsule collapse and regularly broken valve springs. After one of the latter fell into a cylinder, engine No. 15 replaced No. 11. It had been decided at an early stage that the Merlin C would only be used for test purposes, with the developed F variant, later known as the Merlin I, planned for production aircraft.

Undoubtedly influenced by world events, the Air Ministry was very keen to see K5083 make its first scheduled visit to the Aeroplane and Armament Experimental Establishment (A&AEE) at Martlesham Heath. Bulman flew K5083 there on 5 March 1936, the same day the Spitfire made its maiden flight from Eastleigh in the hands of Joseph 'Mutt' Summers. RAF technical officers studied the Hawker with a fine-tooth comb before a designated test pilot was assigned to evaluate the aircraft. This highly responsible task fell upon the experienced shoulders of Sergeant Samuel 'Sammy' Wroath.

Engine problems dogged the fighter at Martlesham, and two further Merlin Cs were fitted. The majority of the snags were rectified after a visit to Rolls-Royce at Hucknall following K5083's return from Martlesham in April 1936.

In the meantime, the Flight Section of the A&AEE had already submitted the results of its trial to the Air Ministry. Some of its details showed that K5083 achieved a maximum speed of 315mph at 16,200ft, and reached 15,000ft in 5 minutes 42 seconds and 20,000ft in 8 minutes 24 seconds. Its service ceiling was estimated at 34,500ft, all of these figures comfortably beyond the original F.36/34 specification. Generally, all of the departments involved in K5083's initial trial were impressed.

It was not long before a steady line of Air Ministry officers began to arrive at Canbury Park Road to discuss when production could begin. Hawker was already involved in Expansion Scheme E, a government order for 500 fighters and 300 bombers to be satisfied by late 1937. It was clear that most of this order was obsolete, but it could not be cancelled because it contained large orders for Gladiators, Hinds, Wellesleys and Whitleys, all of which the RAF needed.

Rather than wait for an Air Ministry decision on the Hurricane, Hawker began subcontracting its commitments. Hector and Audax production was

OPPOSITE Bulman holds station beneath the camera-aircraft during an early flight in K5083 from Brooklands. (John Dibbs)

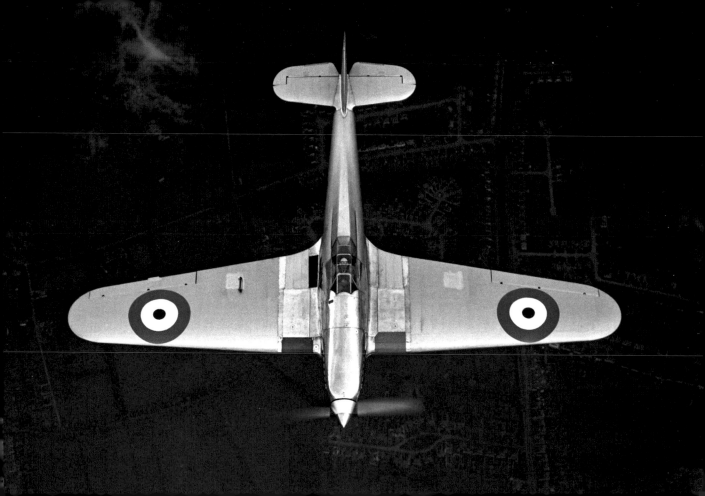

diverted to Westland and that of the Fury II to General Aircraft. The latter was also contracted to carry out Hart and Hind conversions to trainers. This manoeuvring freed 24,000sqft of floor space at Canbury Park Road for new production and 14,000sqft at Brooklands for assembly and finishing.

By May 1936 there was still no Air Ministry production order for the Hurricane, and Hawker decided to begin arrangements at its own risk, starting with the recruitment of 280 skilled machine operators and fitters, and the purchase of the necessary aluminium and steel tubing to produce 1,000 fighters. It was a brave, confident decision.

Hawker notified the Department of Development and Production of its intentions, and the Air Ministry's administrative cogs finally began to turn at speed. Without delay, a draft proposal for Production Scheme F was drawn up and released on 1 June 1936, stating a requirement for 1,000 fighters. On the 3rd, a formal contract, No. 527112/36, was drawn up for 600 'monoplane fighters'. By 8 June,

the fuselage manufacturing drawings had been issued to the production shops. It was not until 27 June 1936, however, that the aircraft was given a proper name, on the same day that it made its first public appearance, at Hendon. Traditionally, fighter aircraft had been given aggressive names including Bulldog, Fury and Gladiator, and Sopwith and Camm chose the name of a violent wind for their latest fighter, the Hurricane.

REFINING THE MERLIN

After the Martlesham trial, modifications revolved around the troublesome engine. Rolls-Royce was hard at work refining the Merlin I while K5083 was refitted with the Merlin C No. 17. Back in the Kingston workshop and dismantled in late July 1936, the prototype had been fitted with fabric-covered, eight-gun wings, and a ring-and-bead gunsight, and the

OPPOSITE The pilot of a Hurricane Mk I turns his plane upside down above the clouds. (Photo by Hulton Archive/Getty Images)

tailplane struts removed. By 17 August, it was at Brooklands again and, after more test flying, prepared for a second visit to Martlesham Heath for final service acceptance trials. However, the Air Ministry was not happy with the Merlin progress.

But the company had already been developing the Merlin G (Merlin II), with a host of modifications including new camshaft mountings, redesigned rocker and valve gear, and improved supercharger bearings. It was therefore decided to divert the Merlin I to the Fairey Battle while the new 1,030hp Merlin II would power the Hurricane and Spitfire. The new engine caused several design issues for Camm, requiring a new nose contour, new radiator fairing and the repositioning of the glycol coolant header tank.

Bulman and test pilot Philip Lucas flew further trials in early November. Now fitted with a new rudder, K5083 was put through a limited spinning trial that revealed an interesting anomaly, resulting in further post-production modifications. Recovery, although easier from a right-hand spin, easily satisfied RAF requirements, but the test pilots were surprised to discover that it was improved when the tailwheel was down. This was noted and the Hurricane delivered to Martlesham in March 1937.

Now it featured eight guns and their ammunition feeds, a radio, redesigned radiator fairing, fixed tailwheel, heavy-duty bulletproof windscreen and sliding canopy. Wroath began his second trial on 3 April on the power of a Merlin C. He had received clear instructions that the performance and handling with regard to the Merlin should not cloud the aircraft's final service report, and the Hurricane passed its service trial with little drama.

The RAF was very happy with how the aircraft performed during a short gun-firing exercise from Eastchurch. It flew 18 live sorties over the range at Leysdown on the Isle of Sheppey, without a stoppage. After visiting all of the RAF's specialist establishments, K5083 was taken on RAF charge at Martlesham Heath on 25 May 1937. It had served Hawker well, but did not represent the forthcoming production variant that was being built in quantity at Kingston.

Sammy Wroath continued to fly K5083 during his tour at Martlesham Heath and, only four days after the aircraft became an RAF machine, he displayed it at the Empire Air Day displays at Felixstowe and Martlesham. It was also put forward as being representative of a modern RAF fighter later in the year, following a request by MGM for an aircraft for the flying sequences in a new film, 1938's *Test Pilot* starring Clark Gable and Myrna Loy.

Little is known of the prototype's history from this point, other than that Wroath flew it several more times during the summer of 1937. His final flight was on 12 October 1937, which, significantly, was the day the first production Hurricane Mk I, L1547, was rolled out of the Brooklands flight shed for its maiden flight, in the hands of Philip Lucas.

OPPOSITE Pilot's decking and engine being installed at the factory of Hawker Aircraft Ltd, June 1938. (Photo by J. A. Hampton/Topical Press Agency/Getty Images)

TECHNICAL SPECIFICATIONS

The Hurricane was a single-engined, single-seat, low-wing monoplane powered by a supercharged, liquid-cooled Merlin V12 inline engine. It was of all-metal construction and its flying surfaces and rear fuselage were fabric-covered, as were the outer wings on early Hurricanes, all later aircraft having metal-covered wings. A retractable undercarriage (including the tailwheel on the very early aircraft only) was fitted, while the standard armament was installed in the wings.

FUSELAGE

The fuselage comprised a metal framework of round tubes shaped to square sections at their ends, where they were bolted together to form boxes, the sides of which formed Warren trusses. Diagonal wires between tubular joints, each with its own screw tensioner, provided further strength, especially in the rear fuselage. The rear fuselage framework included 11 metal frames, tapering rearwards, in which several stringers were attached, the whole covered in doped fabric. No longerons were fitted, since longitudinal strength came from the Warren truss structure.

The forward part of the fuselage used a triangular part-truss layout complete with four engine bearer pads on the upper components. Attached to the forward structure was a line of 'thump-stud' sockets to fix the external engine and ancillary access panels in place.

Behind the cockpit, a large sheet of armour protected the pilot from the rear, while an armoured bulkhead provided protection from the front. A 'break-out' panel on the starboard side of the cockpit below the sliding canopy eased egress in an emergency.

OPPOSITE Factory workers assembling the wing elements of Hawker Hurricane aeroplanes, July 1938. (Photo by Topical Press Agency/Getty Images)

WING CENTRE SECTION

The centre section of the Hurricane's wing was an all-metal twin-spar structure attached to the fuselage via the main Warren trusses. A pair of fuel tanks was located between each main spar, while on the port side the oil tank was positioned at the wing root, ahead of the forward spar.

The undercarriage wells were also located between the main spars, in the lower centre section. The hinge-mounted flaps were attached to the centre section trailing edge on the lower edge of the rear spar. A radiused fillet joint blended the metal-skinned centre section into the fuselage.

OUTER WINGS

Once again, these used a two-spar design, but with a diagonal Warren truss between them and main nose frames along the leading edge; chordwise metal frames created the metal-skinned aerofoil section. The ailerons were hinged to the trailing edge of the rear spar.

Aircraft fitted with cannon did not have Warren trusses, creating more space for access to the weapons, gun bay and ammunition; strength was retained through the installation of secondary spanwise spars.

Strong points were attached to the front and rear spars, inboard of the guns, for fuel tank pylons or bomb racks. Four additional strong points under the spars on later Mk IIs and all Mk IVs accommodated a four-rail rocket projectile (RP) pack.

UNDERCARRIAGE

The retractable undercarriage comprised a single-oleo, semi-pneumatic Vickers strut with a Dunlop or Lockheed wheel mounted on the inboard side. The strut was positioned at the extreme outer edge of the centre section and retracted inwards by a Hawker mechanism actuated by a Dowty hydraulic jack. As the leg retracted, a shortening drag strut pulled the undercarriage aft by seven degrees to clear the main spar before it entered the wheel well.

The wheels were fitted with Dunlop or Lockheed pneumatic brakes as standard and, other than on very early Hurricane Mk Is, the Dowty oleo-sprung lever-suspension tailwheel was non-retractable.

Metal fairing panels were attached to the main undercarriage leg and, once retracted, enclosed the wheel well, with the exception of a small portion of the tyre that remained visible from below. The prototype initially had an additional hinged panel that enclosed the tyre completely, but it was easily fouled on the ground and found to be of little or no aerodynamic advantage and soon deleted.

A lengthened, fixed unit soon replaced the retractable tailwheel of the prototype and early production aircraft.

POWERPLANT

The Rolls-Royce Merlin, originally known as the PV.12, was a single-stage, supercharged, liquid-cooled V12 piston engine. From the Merlin Mk III variant on, the engine had a two-stage supercharger.

Each of the 12 cylinders had two spark plugs and four valves, while the overhead camshafts were driven from the rear. The exhaust manifolds were grouped into pairs per cylinder, with stub-type ejectors.

An 18 Imperial gallon (Imp gal) coolant header tank containing a water/methanol mix was positioned on the upper starboard side of the nose. The large cooling radiator was located in a fairing on the centreline, aft of the landing gear wells. The oil reservoir tank was fitted into the port wing centre section. Air for the carburettor was supplied via an up-draught trunk from an intake to the rear and below the engine.

The propeller reduction gear, positioned on the front of the Merlin, transferred its power to a splined universal propeller shaft. The latter gave the Hurricane the flexibility to use the Rotol, de Havilland or Hamilton Standard three-bladed metal propellers. Aircraft fitted with the Rotol unit also had a constant speed unit at the front of the engine.

THE HURRICANE: MARK BY MARK

HURRICANE MK I

The Hurricane Mk I was in production for more than three years and its early versions differed in many ways from those that left the line later. The aircraft first delivered to 111 Squadron were very basic machines, powered by the Merlin II fitted with a two-bladed Watts fixed-pitch wooden propeller, and featuring fabric-covered outer wings and a ring-and-bead gun sight. They lacked self-sealing fuel tanks and protective armour for the pilot. The aircraft's eight .303in Browning machine guns were positioned outside the propeller arc and therefore did not need synchronisation.

The first batch of aircraft was fitted with a retractable tailwheel, which often jammed in the retracted position.

After further flight testing and experience in service it was agreed that the Mk I needed a larger rudder to improve handling, especially in a spin. As part of the modification, a ventral keel was added to the rear lower fuselage and with it the tailwheel was made fixed. The modification was retrofitted to many early machines and became standard on all subsequent aircraft.

From 1939 onwards, the Merlin III, rated at 1,310hp at 9,000ft, was employed. Fitted with a 'universal' propeller shaft, it initially enabled installation of a de Havilland (Hamilton Standard) three-bladed, two-speed metal propeller, although this interim improvement provided only marginally better performance. Significant enhancement came with the Rotol constant-speed, three-bladed metal propeller, combined with new 'ejector'-type exhausts.

The early Mk I's fabric-covered outer wings were later replaced by metal-skinned units, which also

HURRICANE MK I SPECIFICATION

Powerplant: One 1,030hp Merlin II engine; later a Merlin III rated at 1,310hp at 9,000ft

Length: 31ft 4in (9.53m)

Height (Watts propeller, blades vertical): 13ft 2in (4m)

Wingspan: 40ft (12.2m)

Wing area: 257.6sqft (23.93m²)

Weight (Merlin II): Tare (unladen) 4,743lb (2,151kg); loaded 6,218lb (2,820kg)

Weight (Merlin III): Tare 4,982lb (2,260kg); loaded (Rotol propeller): 6,447lb (2,924kg); loaded (de Havilland two-position propeller): 6,499lb (2,948kg)

Maximum speed at 17,800ft (Merlin III, Rotol propeller): 324mph (521km/h)

Rate of climb at sea level (Merlin III, Rotol propeller): 2,200ft/min

Climb to 20,000ft (Merlin III, Rotol propeller): 8 minutes 6 seconds

Normal range (Merlin III, Rotol propeller): 470 miles (756km)

Absolute ceiling (Merlin III, Rotol propeller): 35,400ft

Armament: 8 × 0.303in Browning machine guns in the wings with 2,660 rounds

saw the gun bay access panels changing shape. By mid-1940, pilot protection was becoming paramount and an armoured-glass panel was fitted into the windscreen, along with 70lb (31.8kg) of armour plate around the cockpit. The fuel tanks in the wing centre section and the forward gravity feed tank forward of the cockpit were also given protection from enemy rounds.

Changes in operational equipment were inevitable. At first these concentrated on the radio, the original TR9 HF type having been replaced by the T/T Type 1133 VHF by mid-1940. Identification friend or foe (IFF) equipment was fitted later in 1940, and a tapered antenna mast replaced the original rod-type unit.

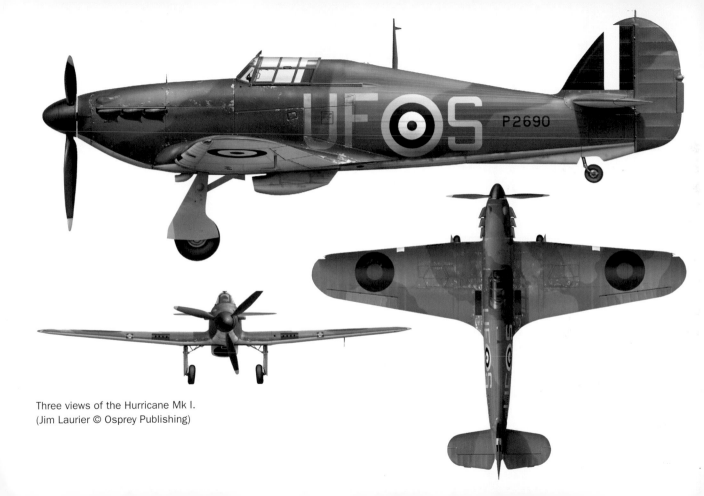

Three views of the Hurricane Mk I.
(Jim Laurier © Osprey Publishing)

The later-build Mk Is saw more air-to-air action than any other Hurricane marks, being at the forefront of the closing stages of the Battle of France in May and June 1940, and through the Battle of Britain from July to October. The Hurricane was popular with its pilots, its turn rate being particularly useful against the Messerschmitt Bf 109E and Bf 110. The Bf 109E was up to 30mph (48km) faster, especially above 15,000ft, but the Hurricane was relatively easy to fly and even in inexperienced hands could still hold its own.

The Mk I Tropical (frequently known as Mk I Trop) variant, designed for operations in hot, dusty climates, also appeared in mid-1940. It featured a large Vokes filter fitted under the nose, filtering air before it passed into the carburettor. The Trop debuted in North Africa and Malta and served in Mediterranean skies through to the war's end.

HURRICANE NF.MK I

A few Mk Is were modified to be more effective as night fighters. They lacked radar and therefore relied on ground control, but were equipped with six-'pot' exhausts and rectangular anti-glare panels ahead of the cockpit to protect the pilot's eyes from the glow of the hot exhausts.

HURRICANE MK I FLOATPLANE

One Hurricane Mk I was part modified (following Drawing No. 13440) with a pair of Blackburn Roc floats. The concept was raised during the Norwegian campaign, but scrapped by June 1940 following the country's fall. The aircraft had a proposed maximum speed of 210mph at 10,000ft.

HILLSON FH.40 SLIP-WING HURRICANE (MK I)

Originally supplied to Canada in late 1938, L1884 served with No. 1 (Royal Canadian Air Force (RCAF)) Squadron as No. 321, before being shipped back to Britain in 1940. On its return, F. Hill and Sons Ltd modified it with a second wing of the same dimensions mounted above the fuselage in a biplane arrangement.

ABOVE A rare photograph of the Slip-Wing Hurricane in flight. (Philip Jarrett)

The extra 'slip-wing' was intended to provide additional lift for a Hurricane overloaded with fuel; it would be jettisoned at cruising altitude. The theory was that Slip-Wing Hurricanes could fly non-stop to Malta or North Africa where fighters were desperately needed, avoiding the costly and dangerous passage by sea.

By the time the project had reached fruition the need for extra aircraft in the Mediterranean theatre had subsided, but the so-called Hillson FH.40 remained at Boscombe Down for trials until January 1944.

SEA HURRICANE MK IA ('HURRICAT')

The Hurricane was a natural choice for the Royal Navy's Fleet Air Arm (FAA), which was desperately in need of modern fighters to operate from its carriers. Compared to the Spitfire, the Hurricane was much easier to handle and its wide-track undercarriage was perfectly suited to carrier landings.

The first FAA Hurricanes were standard Mk Is transferred directly from the RAF, but in November 1940 the need for specialised aircraft was recognised. The idea was to build Fighter Catapult Ships (FCS) each carrying a pair of 'expendable' Hurricanes that would be launched when an enemy aircraft had been sighted. The new fighter was designated Sea Hurricane Mk IA and modified with catapult spools, FAA-standard radio equipment and around 80 other minor changes. Thirty-five aircraft were ordered at

first, with Hawker, Gloster or General Aircraft performing the conversions. It was General Aircraft that ultimately completed the majority of Sea Hurricane modifications – no Sea Hurricanes were built as such, all were conversions of standard production Hurricanes.

While the FCS were crewed by Royal Navy sailors and their aircraft flown by FAA pilots, the Sea Hurricanes were also flown from Catapult Aircraft Merchantmen (CAM), crewed by civilians and with RAF pilots doing the flying.

Operating a Sea Hurricane from these merchantmen was a 'one-way only' operation, since there was no facility to recover the aircraft after it was launched. If it was not in range of an airfield, the pilot had only two options: bail out or ditch the aircraft near an Allied ship. The latter was particularly hazardous because of the Hurricane's large under-belly radiator intake, which dug into the water on touchdown and pitched the fighter down, often sending it under the surface almost instantly.

The first successful operation involving a Sea Hurricane Mk IA occurred on 2 August 1941 when Lieutenant Commander R. W. H. Everett was launched from the FCS HMS *Maplin*. His quarry was a Focke-Wulf Fw 200 Condor, which, after a very long chase during which he avoided as much of its defensive fire as possible, he set on fire to crash into the sea a few minutes later. Everett's Sea Hurricane had taken several hits and was losing oil, so he decided to take to his parachute instead of risking a ditching.

But the fighter had other ideas. Everett made several attempts to bail out with the aircraft inverted, but the Sea Hurricane kept pitching down, forcing him back into his seat. Left with no option but to ditch, Everett came down near an Allied destroyer, only for the fighter to pitch into the sea and disappear below the waves. Although not the strongest of swimmers,

OPPOSITE Sea Hurricane Mk IB (Z4039) of No. 762 Squadron, in flight, 1943. (Photo by Charles E. Brown/Royal Air Force Museum/Getty Images)

Everett managed to drag himself to the surface and was rescued a few moments later. He was awarded the Distinguished Service Order (DSO) for becoming the first pilot to destroy an Fw 200 using a catapult Sea Hurricane.

SEA HURRICANE MK IB

The first dedicated FAA Sea Hurricane was the Mk IB, fitted with catapult spools and an arrestor hook for operation from aircraft carriers. The first example was a Canadian-built Mk I (later designated Mk X), P5187, which first flew as a Sea Hurricane Mk IB in March 1941.

Full production began from May 1941 and by October, 120 Mk IBs had been completed, although this total included several early Hurricane Mk IIAs and Mk IIBs, plus a handful of Canadian-built Mk X, XI and XII aircraft, making the exact definition of a Sea Hurricane IB very difficult. The general consensus is that it was any Hurricane that 'possessed an arrestor hook and whose gun armament did not protrude forward of the wing leading edge'. This reference to armament was introduced when the Admiralty ordered 100 Merlin III-powered Sea Hurricane Mk IBs to be re-armed with 20mm Hispano cannon; this variant was subsequently designated Mk IC.

By the end of 1941, the FAA could boast four squadrons of Sea Hurricane Mk IBs.

SEA HURRICANE MK IC

The Sea Hurricane Mk IC employed standard Hurricane Mk IIC wings fitted to a Mk I fuselage. Its obvious difference compared to earlier Sea Hurricanes was its prominent 20mm Hispano cannon, of which it had a pair in each wing. It also featured catapult spools, an arrestor hook and other naval equipment.

Powered by a 1,030hp Merlin III, the heavily armed Sea Hurricane Mk IC managed 296mph at 15,000ft. Operational off the Royal Navy's carriers from early 1942, it was a vast improvement over the Fairey Fulmar.

HURRICANE I GUNS

The Hurricane I boasted four Browning 0.303-in machine guns in each wing. Re-arming a Hurricane I usually took a two-man team 30 minutes. Each Browning was loaded with 332 rounds of ammunition which, at 20 rounds per second, would last just 17 seconds. The magazines were grouped together in a single bay in each wing and accessible from above, allowing them to be replenished more quickly than those of the Spitfire. Although the Brownings were very reliable, they were regularly criticised by RAF pilots for not providing enough punch when it came to shooting down German fighters and bombers.

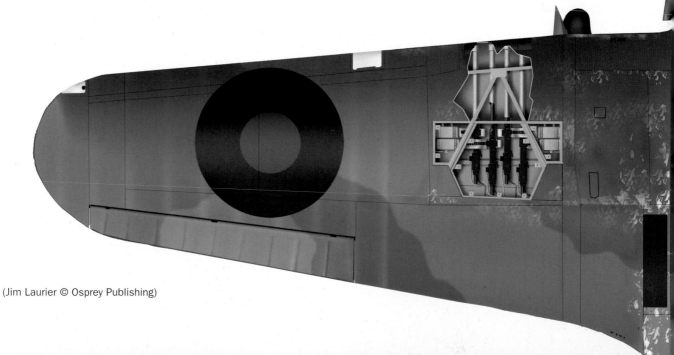

(Jim Laurier © Osprey Publishing)

HURRICANE MK II

With the arrival of the Merlin XX engine, Camm was given the opportunity to improve the Hurricane's performance without carrying out time-consuming and costly modifications to the airframe. The Merlin XX featured a two-speed supercharger, selected by the pilot depending upon altitude. Above 18,000ft, the pilot could select 'Full Supercharger' rating, which gave the Hurricane a top speed of 339mph at 22,000ft, almost on a par with the Bf 109E. At lower altitudes, 'Moderate Supercharger' rating was selected, optimising performance at that level. Ironically, however, as the Mk II was being introduced, the Hurricane was moving increasingly into the low-level fighter-bomber role and the advantage of the Merlin XX was not fully exploited.

OPPOSITE A combat-weary 'Hurribomber' of No 607 Sqn has a single 250lb bomb secured to its two underwing pylons. Note the blanked-off port for the missing 0.303-in machine gun in the starboard wing – the corresponding weapon in the port wing was also deleted. To the right of the inboard guns is the gun ciné camera, installed within the leading edge of the starboard wing. (John Dibbs)

To help accommodate the new engine and its ancillary equipment, the Hurricane's forward centre section was lengthened by a few inches, while the carburettor air intake was moved aft 3in. Rather than the pure glycol used to cool the earlier Merlins, the XX required a glycol/water mix of 30 to 70 per cent, helping ease the pressure on production of this valuable commodity. A larger radiator was required and a new circular oil cooler was designed.

The Mk II became the most built of all Hurricane marks, beginning with the prototype, converted Mk I P3269, first flown on 11 June 1940. As with the previous mark, the lengthy production of the Mk II saw several subtle modifications made, including installation of a new tailwheel leg and a modified spinner.

The Mk II began to arrive en masse with RAF squadrons during the closing stages of the Battle of Britain in the autumn of 1940, when Hawker was receiving massive production orders for the new fighter. Number 605 (County of Warwick) Squadron at Croydon was first to receive the Mk II, from November 1940.

HURRICANE MK IIA

The earliest Mk IIs were little more than Mk Is with the Merlin XX engine. Still sporting the original eight machine gun arrangement, at first they were designated Mk IIA Series I. Aircraft built with modified wings had provision for an additional pair of machine guns in each outer wing section and were officially designated Mk IIA Series II. However, insufficient Brownings were available to meet demand and the Series II flew with the regular eight-gun fit in service.

HURRICANE MK IIB

With the Mk IIB, the 12-gun fit was finally successfully expressed, but the additional weight outboard naturally affected the aircraft's handling and some pilots had the two outermost weapons removed. Others had all four deleted, effectively reducing their aircraft to Mk IIA standard.

In May 1941, trials with underwing hardpoints capable of mounting a 250lb bomb showed the Hurricane's ground-attack potential, and production of a modified Mk IIB variant equipped for a weapon of up to 500lb under each wing, or a long-range fuel tank, was put in hand. The bomb-armed Hurricane was soon nicknamed 'Hurribomber' and became useful in operations over Northern Europe, in many ways paving the way for its stablemate, the Typhoon.

Number 56 Squadron at North Weald in Essex was the first unit to receive the Mk IIB, in February 1941, flying it alongside the Typhoon from September and retaining it until March 1942. By the middle of 1941, Mk IIBs were serving with 20 RAF squadrons.

THE LAMINAR FLOW MK IIB

After serving with Nos. 17, 123, 132 (twice), 331, 43 and 245 Squadrons, Hurricane Mk IIB Z3687 was donated to the Royal Aircraft Establishment (RAE), where it began a new career testing the Armstrong Whitworth laminar-flow wing. Painted all white and highly polished with even its roundels removed, the aircraft was used to investigate airflow over the wings.

Testing continued throughout 1944 and 1945, but it remained on RAE charge and was used as a hack until at least 1948. The exact date when Z3687 was grounded is unknown, but it was officially struck off charge (SOC) on 9 April 1951, by which time it was residing at 22 MU (Maintenance Unit), Silloth. Here, several major components were removed to keep Mk IIC LF363 flying; then operating from Waterbeach, today it serves the Royal Air Force Battle of Britain Memorial Flight (BBMF).

HURRICANE MK IIC

The rifle-calibre .303in machine gun lacked the punch to knock down a heavily armoured enemy aircraft without multiple hits, and enemy bombers often limped back home during the Battle of Britain after a Hurricane or Spitfire had exhausted its ammunition against them. Cannon were the solution and the 20mm Hispano was trialled during the Battle of Britain.

In the Hurricane Mk IIC, four 20mm Hispano cannon (two in each wing) replaced the machine guns; up to 364 rounds of ammunition could be carried. The Hurricane was thus transformed into a formidable ground-attack aircraft and one that could tackle enemy aircraft more effectively, especially during intruder operations by day and night. A few aircraft were built with Oerlikon cannon as an alternative to the Hispano; some were retrofitted with the latter weapon in service and the Oerlikon Hurricanes were never widespread.

A pair of 250lb or 500lb bombs could be carried, or a pair of long-range fuel tanks. The first Mk IICs were delivered to No. 3 Squadron at Martlesham Heath from April 1941, before it moved to Hunsdon, via Stapleford Tawney, in August. Numbers 1, 3, 87, 247 and 257 Squadrons quickly became Mk IIC night intruder specialists over Northern France and the Low Countries. Number 1 Squadron in particular, operating from Tangmere, built an excellent record thanks to a pair of expert night-fighting tacticians, Squadron

Mk IIC BE500, the personal aircraft of Squadron leader D. G. Smallwood during his tour as commanding officer of 87 squadron. BE500 served with 533 Squadron and in the Far East before being SOC in August 1944. (Adam Tooby © Osprey Publishing)

Leader J. MacLachlan and Flight Lieutenant 'Kut' Kuttelwascher.

The Mk IIC continued on offensive operations into 1942, Nos. 3, 43, 87 and 245 Squadrons all taking part in the historic Dieppe raid on 19 August 1942. The mark remained in frontline service with No. 309 Squadron in the defence of Scotland until 1944, the Mustang replacing it in October.

SEA HURRICANE MK IIC

By far the best of the naval Hurricanes, the Sea Hurricane Mk IIC was furnished with the standard catapult spools, arrestor hook and naval radio equipment. Taking full advantage of the Merlin XX engine, it was very popular with FAA pilots and by early 1944 more than 400 had been converted from Hurricane Mk IIC standard.

HURRICANE MK II SPECIFICATION

Powerplant (Hurricane and Sea Hurricane Mk IIC): One Rolls-Royce Merlin XX rated at 1,280hp for take-off and 1,850hp at 21,000ft

Length: 32ft (9.75m)

Height: 13ft 3in (4.04m)

Wingspan: 40ft (12.90m)

Wing area: 257.6sqft (23.93m²)

Weight (Mk IIB): Tare 5,467lb (2,480kg); loaded 7,233lb (3,281kg)

Weight (Mk IIB Trop): Tare 5,594lb (2,537kg); loaded 7,233lb (3,281kg)

Weight (Mk IIC): Tare 5,658lb (2,566kg); loaded 7,396lb (3,355kg)

Weight (Mk IIC Trop): Tare 5,785lb (2,624kg); loaded 7,544lb (3,422kg)

Weight (Sea Hurricane Mk IIC): Tare 5,738lb (2,603kg); loaded 7,618lb (3,455kg)

Weight (Mk IID Trop): Tare 5,550lb (2,517kg); loaded 7,850lb (3,561kg)

Maximum speed (Mk IIC at 22,000ft): 339mph (546km/h)

Climb to 20,000ft (Mk IIC): 9 minutes 6 seconds

Standard range (Mk IIC): 460 miles (747km)

Range with auxiliary tanks (Mk IIC): 970 miles (1,561km)

Service ceiling (Mk IIC): 32,400ft

Armament: Mk II and Mk IIA 8 × .303in machine guns; Mk IIB 12 × .303in machine-guns; later provision for two 250 or two 500lb bombs; Mk IIC 4 × 20mm Hispano cannon in the wings and provision to carry up to two 500lb bombs; Mk IID 2 × Vickers Type 'S' 40mm cannon and one or two .303in machine guns

HURRICANE MK IID

As the war progressed, the need for an aircraft capable of attacking enemy tanks and other vehicles emerged, especially in the North African desert. On the ground, German armour had a distinct advantage against all contemporary Allied tanks, but the tide might be turned if a large calibre weapon could be used against them from above.

The Hurricane Mk IID was specially equipped for the role, fitted with a Vickers Type 'S' 40mm cannon in a pod under each wing, with two (sometimes reduced to one) tracer-armed .303in machine guns retained for sighting. The prototype, ex-Mk IIA Z2326, was first flown in its new form in September 1941.

The Mk IID 'tank-buster' entered service with No. 6 Squadron in April 1942 at Bu Amud, near Tobruk. It took the type into action for the first time on 6 June 1942 and enjoyed great success against General Rommel's armour, soon gaining the nickname the 'Flying Tin-opener' for its ability to 'open up' a tank.

The Mk IID was a rare machine in Britain, only serving with Nos. 164 and 184 Squadrons, but was more prolific in the Far East, proving particularly useful in Burma.

HURRICANE MK IIE

Incorporating further wing modifications, the proposed Mk IIE was considered too far evolved from the Mk II to be a subvariant and was therefore redesignated as the Mk IV.

HURRICANE MK III

The Mk III was intended as a contingency should the supply of Rolls-Royce Merlin engines fail to meet demand. It was designed to accept the US-built Packard Merlin, but by the time production was to have begun the British-built engine was readily available. The Packard was, however, installed in the 1,451 Mk X, XI and XII Hurricanes built in Canada.

OPPOSITE A Hurricane Mk IV of No. 6 Squadron being serviced on an airfield in Italy. Note the 44-gallon long-range fuel tank under the port wing, and four 3-inch rocket projectiles under the starboard – also the Type G45 gun camera being serviced by the airman standing second from the right. (© IWM CNA 3035)

HURRICANE MK IV

Power: One 1,620hp Merlin 24 or 27 engine

Dimensions: As Mk II

Weight: Tare 6,150lb (2,790kg); loaded 8,462lb (3,838kg)

Performance: As per Mk IID; but maximum speed at 13,500ft with eight 60lb RPs and 350lb of armour 284mph (457km/h)

Armament: 2 × 0.303in Browning guns in the wings, plus provision for 2 × 40mm Vickers Type 'S' guns, 8 × 60lb RPs or 2 × 250 or 500lb bombs

HURRICANE MK IV

Although the last Hurricanes to leave the production line were Mk IICs, the final production variant was the Mk IV, marking the Hurricane's full evolution from pure fighter to ground attack. A 'universal' wing, planned for the Mk IIE, expanded the variety of available stores. These included the 40mm cannon of the Mk IID, as well as RPs, 250 and 500lb bombs, and long-range fuel tanks. Protective armour was also increased, with 350lb positioned around the cockpit, radiator, fuel tanks and engine. The latter was a 1,620hp Merlin 24 or 27 fitted with a Vokes filter.

The Mk IV served with 26 operational RAF squadrons, arriving in strength from the spring of 1943. The majority served in Tunisia and northwards through Italy, and in the Far East, where the Mk IV flew fighter escort duties, photographic and fighter reconnaissance and general ground-attack operations. The latter in particular saw the combined efforts of Mk IIDs and Mk IVs decimate Japanese armour, ground transport and river craft during the final assault on Rangoon.

Number 6 Squadron received the Mk IV from July 1943, and after remaining in Italy until the war's end, took its aircraft to Palestine where, in February 1946, some of the longest serving Hurricanes were retired in favour of the Spitfire.

HURRICANE MK V

Power: One 1,645hp Merlin 32 engine

Dimensions: As Mk II

All-up weight: 9,300lb (4,218kg)

Maximum speed: 326mph (525km/h) at 500ft

Armament: As Mk IV

HURRICANE MK V

The Mk V was an attempt to stretch the Hurricane's ground-attack capability one stage further, with the intention of producing an optimised aircraft for operations in the Far East. Powered by the Merlin 32 engine driving a Rotol four-bladed propeller, the Mk V was built to the extent of just three examples during 1943, two of them as Mk IV conversions.

Despite having an all-up weight of 9,300lb, the Mk V was capable of flying at 326mph at 500ft, although there was no significant improvement in general performance compared to the Mk IIC.

The Air Ministry ultimately decided that the large stocks of Hurricanes already available in India would suffice and the Mk V was never developed beyond the prototypes.

PHOTOGRAPHIC RECONNAISSANCE
HURRICANE PR.MK I

As many as 20 unarmed Hurricane PR.Mk I reconnaissance conversions may have been completed at Heliopolis, Egypt, with additional fuel tanks in their gun bays after some, perhaps all, guns were removed. At least three conversions are known in relative detail, DG613 featuring a fan of three 14in F.24 cameras and V7423 and V7428 mounting pairs of 8in F.24 cameras. A fairing on the fuselage underside aft of the wing covered the protruding camera lens barrels. It should be noted that Rolls-Royce had already modified DG613 from Mk I to Mk IIA standard prior to the work carried out in Egypt and hence this aircraft at least ought really to have been designated as a PR.Mk IIA.

HURRICANE PR.MK II

Eighteen PR.Mk II Hurricanes were converted from Mk IIA airframes. It seems likely they were all tropicalised and equipped for their new role similarly to the PR.Mk I.

HURRICANE PR.MK IIB AND PR.MK IIC

The PR.Mk IIB and PR.Mk IIC aircraft were converted from Hurricane Mk IIB and Mk IIC stock.

HURRICANE TACR.MK I AND TACR.MK II (FE)

Number 103 MU at Aboukir modified eight Hurricane Mk Is for tactical reconnaissance by fitting a single vertically mounted F.24 camera. The MU also converted several repaired Mk IIAs and Mk IIBs during 1941, the modified machines being redesignated as TacR.Mk IIs. Modified Mk IICs serving in the Far East were designated TacR.Mk II (FE). The TacRs were variously unarmed, retained the full complement of Brownings or flew with only two or four.

MADE IN CANADA

As early as 1937, senior RCAF staff attempted to acquire Hurricanes but met with objections from the Air Ministry, which was uncertain whether the RAF would have sufficient numbers for its own purposes. Political manoeuvring and continuous pressure from Canada, especially at the time of the Munich Crisis in 1938, saw the British government come round to the idea of equipping Commonwealth squadrons with Hurricanes that could fly in support of the RAF in the event of a war.

By October 1938, the first five of 20 allocated Hurricane Mk Is had been diverted from the Kingston production line for shipment to Canada. At the same time, a further agreement to produce the fighter in

OPPOSITE The vast majority of Canadian-built Hurricanes were fitted with Hamilton-Standard three-bladed metal propellers manufactured locally under license rather than the Rotol or de Havilland propellers favoured in Britain. The hub change mechanism for the American-designed propeller proved to be too large for the Rotol or de Havilland spinners so it was simply left uncovered. This unidentified Hurricane XII of No. 135 (F) Squadron was photographed at Patricia Bay on 10 November 1942. (Mark Peapell)

Canada had been achieved, with production to be undertaken by the Canadian Car and Foundry Company in Montreal. On 2 March 1939 a single pattern Hurricane was shipped to Canada, and in a very short period of time production lines were set up, thanks to efforts on both sides of the Atlantic. By 1940, the first of 1,451 Canadian-built Hurricanes had left the production line at Montreal.

HURRICANE MK I

The first 40 Hurricanes built by the Canadians were standard Mk Is powered by the Merlin III engine and fitted with de Havilland propellers.

HURRICANE MK X

The Mk X was fitted with a 1,390hp Packard-Merlin 28 and fitted with a Hamilton Standard propeller. One hundred were produced with an eight-gun wing while the remaining 389 had the Mk IIB wing. A large quantity was later converted to have the Mk IIC wing and of those subsequently shipped to Britain, all were modified to Mk IIB and Mk IIC standard. The 489 Mk Xs were built during 1940 and 1941.

Several Hurricane Mk Xs were fitted with fixed skis replacing their main landing gear and a 'snow-shoe' tailskid. All the original undercarriage components were removed and their apertures faired over. The modified aircraft served only with the RCAF, from 1941 to 1943.

HURRICANE MK XI AND MK XIB

The Mk XI was fitted with 12-gun armament and the Mk XIB with four cannon. The majority of the 150 aircraft built were shipped to the Soviet Union.

HURRICANE MK XII

The Mk XII introduced the 1,300hp Packard-Merlin 29 engine and Mk IIC modifications. Armament was as for the Mk XI. There were 248 aircraft built.

OPPOSITE Airmen from the No. 402 'Winnipeg Bears' Squadron of the Royal Canadian Air Force run to their Hawker Hurricane fighter planes at RAF Digby, Lincolnshire, 21 April 1941. (Photo by Parker/Fox Photos/Getty Images)

SEA HURRICANE MK XIIA

The Sea Hurricane Mk XIIA was similar to the Mk XII, but with an eight-gun wing, catapult spools and arrestor hook.

TWO-SEATERS

A two-seat Hurricane might have been a valuable asset for the RAF prior to World War II. However, only the Persian and Russian air forces and, perhaps surprisingly, the US Army Air Force, operated such aircraft.

Ten Hurricanes were modified as trainers for the Russians, with a second cockpit and dual controls to help pilots convert to the hundreds of machines of the type that were flooding into the country. These hard working aircraft also served as glider tugs for A-7 and G-11 gliders, towing them on several operations. One aircraft, BW945, doubled as an artillery spotter, with a single machine gun mounted in the rear cockpit.

Three aircraft used as target tugs for the USAAF's 350th Fighter Group in Sardinia during 1944, including LB460, were also modified as two-seaters.

The second cockpit was enclosed by skilful use of a second sliding canopy that mated with the original.

Two trainers for the Persian Air Force first flew with open cockpits in 1946, but before delivery the rear cockpit was enclosed with a Hawker Tempest hood. The initial example, ex-Hurricane Mk IIC KZ232, was first flown from Langley on 27 September 1946 and by early 1947 both aircraft, now designated T.Mk IIC and serialled 2-31 and 2-32, were in service.

PROPOSALS

F.37/35 FOUR-CANNON DESIGN

Tendered on 23 April 1936, F.37/35 was based on the Hurricane prototype but fitted with four 20mm Oerlikon cannon. It was rejected in favour of the Westland Whirlwind.

TWO-CANNON HURRICANE

The two-cannon Hurricane evolved from a trial installation of two 20mm Oerlikon cannon mounted under the wings and additional cockpit armour during service trials in 1939. One aircraft successfully served with No. 151 Squadron during the Battle of Britain.

YUGOSLAV DAIMLER-BENZ HURRICANE

The Daimler-Benz Hurricane was planned for production with a DB601A engine in Yugoslavia. One aircraft was completed under licence before the German invasion of April 1941.

DAGGER HURRICANE

Installation of the Napier Dagger engine was proposed to ease pressure on Merlin production. The concept was studied in detail during the Battle of Britain period but had been shelved by November 1940.

GRIFFON HURRICANE

A Rolls-Royce Griffon IIA-powered F.37/35 version was proposed in 1939–41. The concept was dropped when the Typhoon entered production.

HERCULES HURRICANE

The Bristol Hercules was proposed as another Hurricane powerplant option in 1941. Under the concept, all second-line Hurricanes could be fitted with the more prolific Bristol unit to ease pressure on Merlin production.

SIDE-BLISTER CANOPY

The side-blister canopy did not appear in production, but at least one No. 145 Squadron aircraft was flown with it in mid-1940.

HURRICANE (IMPROVED CANOPY) PROJECT

The improved canopy project modified the lower rear fuselage and employed a one-piece canopy to help improve field of vision. One prototype was built, but trials had ceased by March 1942.

COMBAT OPERATIONS

The honour of receiving the RAF's first monoplane fighter was bestowed upon No. 111 Squadron, under the command of Squadron Leader J. W. Gillan, in December 1937. The official 'start date' for re-equipping from its Gaunt lets was 1 January 1938, but four Hurricanes, L1548 to L1551, had already arrived at Northolt, Middlesex, before Christmas Day 1937.

By the end of February 1938, the full squadron establishment of 16 aircraft had arrived, making up two flights of six and four in reserve. The task now facing No. 111 Squadron's pilots was that of converting from the 230mph Gauntlet, with its open cockpit and fixed undercarriage, to the 330mph Hurricane, with its enclosed cockpit, flaps and retractable undercarriage.

OPPOSITE Hurricane Mk Is (L1555, L1558, L1560, L1564 and others) of No. 111 Squadron, Northolt, 1938. (Photo by Charles E. Brown/Royal Air Force Museum/Getty Images)

RECORD-BREAKING FLIGHT

Gillan was well aware that his pilots needed a confidence booster, especially after one was killed in a flying accident, even though it was through no fault of the aircraft. Gillan started planning a high-speed flight between Northolt and Turnhouse (near Edinburgh) for 10 February 1938. Flying L1555, he set course for Turnhouse in the early afternoon, but after encountering a strong headwind almost all the way, did not land at the Scottish airfield until 1600hrs. It was obvious to Gillan that the headwind would be a beneficial tailwind on the return flight to Northolt if he could refuel and take-off again quickly.

Having done so, Gillan climbed to 17,000ft as dusk began to descend and set course for Northolt above heavy clouds and without oxygen. A break in the cloud revealed the twinkling lights of Bedford below, and Gillan began a shallow descent through the gap. He arrived over Northolt alarmed by the fact that his ground speed was well over 450mph, but slowed to land successfully, taxiing across Northolt's grass having covered the 327 miles from Turnhouse in just 48 minutes, at an average speed of 408.75mph. The flight had been flown at full throttle and the Merlin engine had not faltered.

Once the national and world press got hold of the story, No. 111 Squadron's pilots were elevated to the RAF elite. The Air Ministry kept quiet about the 80mph tailwind of which Gillan had taken advantage, but which earned him the service nickname 'Downwind Gillan'. His aim had simply been to instil confidence in his young pilots and there is no doubt he achieved this in style – 'Treble One' was never the same again. Gillan's approach to training his pilots and his leadership by example was later recognised with the award of the AFC.

MORE SQUADRONS

The next unit to receive the Hurricane was No. 3 Squadron, under the command of Squadron Leader H. L. P. Lester. Having operated the Bulldog through most of the 1930s and then briefly the Gladiator, No. 3 Squadron received its first Hurricanes at Kenley, Surrey from March 1938. It was not a large airfield and since the Hurricane required considerably more space than the biplanes that preceded it, a spate of accidents occurred as pilots struggled to keep the modern fighter within the airfield boundary. The problem came to a head in May, when two Hurricanes were written off and Pilot Officer H. Henry-May was killed when L1579 stalled on approach and dived into the ground.

A quick decision saw No. 3 Squadron re-equip with the Gladiator while Kenley was expanded to cope

OPPOSITE Eleven Hurricanes of 'Treble One' with their engines running are about to taxi out to begin the day's flying demonstration for the press at Northolt in 1938. Worthy of note here is the unique way that '111' has been unofficially painted on the rear fuselage in at least three different ways. Squadron Leader J. W. Gillan is also visible in the fourth aircraft along, L1555, which is complete with squadron leader's flash below the cockpit. (Bettman/Getty Images)

with the new fighter. The Hurricane did not return to No. 3 Squadron until July 1939, by which time the unit had moved to nearby Biggin Hill.

From 1 April, squadron strength was increased to 20 or 21 aircraft, arranged as two flights of nine aircraft each, with two or sometimes three machines used for conversion training. Under this new regime, the third Hurricane unit became No. 56 Squadron, based at North Weald under the command of Squadron Leader C. L. Lea-Cox. The unit had also operated the Gladiator before its first Hurricanes were delivered in May and June 1938. The transition to the monoplane was carried out with few problems and in August, No. 56 Squadron was declared operational with the Hurricane.

By the time of the Munich Crisis in September 1938, Fighter Command's plans ought to have seen at least a dozen squadrons of Hurricanes and Spitfires operational.

OPPOSITE Watched by ground crew, the 'A' Flight of No. 56 Squadron sets out for France in May 1940 during the height of the Blitzkrieg. (John Dibbs)

In reality, Nos. 56 and 111 Squadrons were the only Hurricane units that could be brought to readiness, while Spitfires were just arriving on No. 19 Squadron, and at a slow rate. The latter continued to be delivered slowly through the remainder of 1938, but the pace of Hurricane delivery began to accelerate. By October, the rate of production of the Hurricane was high enough to re-equip one squadron per month and replace any losses incurred by units already receiving the type.

The next Hurricane squadrons formed were both based at Debden in Essex. First was No. 87 Squadron under the command of Squadron Leader J. Rhys-Jones, which saw its Gladiators replaced from July 1938 onwards. The transition period from biplane to monoplane would have been quicker if No. 87 Squadron had not been ordered to donate its 'A' Flight as a nucleus for the second Hurricane unit at Debden, No. 85 Squadron.

Re-formed on 1 June, No. 85 Squadron used the Gladiator for a few months before its Hurricanes began arriving in September. It was not until

November that it was officially recognised as an operational unit, now under the command of Squadron Leader D. F. W. Atcherley.

Number 73 Squadron, under the command of Squadron Leader E. S. Finch and based at Digby in Lincolnshire, had begun receiving the new fighters in late July 1938. Number 32 Squadron at Biggin Hill, commanded by Squadron Leader R. Pyne DFC, followed in September, then it was the turn of three Tangmere-based squadrons. Squadron Leader I. A. Bertram's No.1 Squadron replaced its Gladiators in October, followed by Nos. 43 and 79 Squadrons, under the command of Squadron Leaders R. E. Bain and G. D. Emms respectively, which received their Hurricanes in November. Before the year was over, the Gauntlets of No. 151 Squadron, under the command of Squadron Leader E. M. Donaldson at North Weald, were also replaced.

By the end of 1938, five Hurricane squadrons were operational and five more were waiting in the wings. The Spitfire, by contrast, had only been delivered to Nos. 19 and 66 Squadrons, neither of which was operational.

Deliveries continued apace into 1939, the first unit of the year being Squadron Leader J. H. Edwardes-Jones's No. 213 Squadron at Wittering in Northamptonshire, which had been flying the Gauntlet since its re-formation in March 1937. Digby-based No. 46 Squadron, under the command of Squadron Leader P. Barwell, received its first Hurricanes in late February 1939.

Much to the surprise of the regular air force, let alone the auxiliaries themselves, No. 501 (County of Gloucester) Squadron of the Auxiliary Air Force (AAF), based at Filton near Bristol under the charge of Squadron Leader M. V. M. Clube, received Hurricanes from March to replace its ageing Hinds. A second auxiliary unit, No. 504 (County of Nottingham) Squadron, under Squadron Leader Sir H. M. Seely Bt MP received Hurricanes at Hucknall from May.

THE PHONEY WAR

The first few months of the war in Western Europe were known as the 'Phoney War'. It was a period of calm before the storm as Germany regrouped after its invasion of Poland and Allied commanders braced themselves for the inevitable Blitzkrieg. Nevertheless, the RAF Hurricanes took part in operations in mainland Europe.

Just three days after the first German troops crossed the Polish border on 1 September 1939, Britain and France declared war. In a prearranged agreement with France, Britain quickly established the British Expeditionary Force (BEF), which crossed the Channel and took up position along the French border with Belgium. The RAF contributed two large groups to form the Air Component of the BEF and the Advanced Air Striking Force (AASF). Among the many squadrons contained within the Air Component, Nos. 85 and 87 squadrons flew Hurricanes, while the AASF contained Nos. 1 and 73 Squadrons, tasked with flying escort operations in support of Blenheim and Battle squadrons, and general air defence.

Pressure began to build for at least another six fighter squadrons to be deployed, but Air Chief Marshal Hugh Dowding, head of Fighter Command, fervently resisted sending more of his precious aircraft. However, he compromised by despatching a pair of auxiliary units, Nos. 607 and 615 Squadrons, both flying the Gladiator, which arrived in France in November 1939. Dowding also promised to reconsider his decision if the Germans launched a major offensive, if the BEF was left in a perilous position or if, most crucially, Fighter Command's strength reached the commander-in-chief's minimum figure of 52 operational squadrons.

After initial high hopes of seeing action, the pilots of No. 1 Squadron at Vassincourt, No. 73 Squadron at Rouvres, and Nos. 85 and 87 Squadrons at Lille/Seclin found themselves flying the odd patrol and occasional scramble. For the RAF, the main enemy during autumn and winter 1939–40 was the weather, since after a large amount of rain and snow it was not long before the badly drained French airfields turned to mud. Nonetheless, the sturdiness of the Hurricane and its excellent wide-track undercarriage meant that it was very unusual for operations to be disrupted.

With its motto *In omnibus princeps* (first in all things), it was appropriate that No. 1 Squadron was first to shoot down an enemy aircraft. On 30 October 1939, Pilot Officer P. Mould, in L1842, attacked and shot down a Dornier Do 17P over Toul at 18,000ft. L1842 was in action again on 23 November, this time in the hands of Sergeant A. V. 'Taffy' Clowes. Clowes was one of three in a section led by Flight Lieutenant G. Plinston when they attacked a lone Heinkel He 111 at 20,000ft between Metz and Verdun. All three pilots attacked the bomber, but it was Clowes who delivered the final, fatal blow. As Clowes pulled away following his attack, half a dozen French Morane-Saulnier fighters joined the fray. In their excitement, one of the French pilots collided with L1842, removing half its rudder and one elevator. Clowes managed to maintain control and carry out a forced landing at Vassincourt, where the Hurricane was repaired in situ.

In the meantime, No. 73 Squadron had also been quick off the mark, when Flying Officer E. J. 'Cobber' Kain claimed the unit's first kill on 2 November. Number 85 Squadron followed on 21 November when Flight Lieutenant R. Lee in L1898 shot down an He 111 off Boulogne. Before the month was over, No. 87 Squadron had caught up, when Flight Lieutenant R. Jeff destroyed another He 111 near Hazebrouck.

By now, the last of 600 L-series Hurricanes had been delivered, all built at Brooklands (these aircraft had serial numbers prefixed 'L'). Another batch of 300 aircraft followed without disruption to the production line.

Flying from Acklington in Northumberland, 111 Squadron achieved its first success with the Hurricane. Only days before departing for Drem in East Lothian, the commanding officer, Squadron Leader H. Broadhurst AFC, took off alone after receiving a report that enemy aircraft were approaching the coast. The weather was atrocious but Broadhurst

pressed on, flying only on instruments through thick cloud. On clearing his iced-up windscreen, he spotted a group of Kampfgeschwader (KG) 26 He 111s inbound from their base in Schleswig.

Broadhurst picked out a single aircraft at a range of 500 yards; the bomber dived into cloud, but Broadhurst remained focused and continued to close until he was just 150 yards from the Heinkel. A quick burst of fire put the ventral gunner out of action, and the second burst sent the Heinkel into a flaming spiral dive into the sea. The first of No. 111 Squadron's many victories, it seemed appropriate that it fell to the popular CO. Broadhurst was awarded the DFC for his action that day in preferring to risk himself rather than his squadron.

THE WINTER WAR

On 30 November 1939 another conflict broke out in Europe, as Finland refused to give in to Russia's demands to build military bases on its soil. The Russians were also calling for a repositioning of the Karelian Isthmus border. This would dissolve the effectiveness of the Mannerheim Line, Finland's only significant line of defence against its much larger neighbour.

Finland's air force, despite being small, was equipped with modern aircraft. The Finns used these well, inflicting heavy losses on Russia's comparatively obsolete air force. Britain was politically in support of Finland's fight against the Soviets, but was slow to provide any kind of military hardware. However, an order already placed by the Finns for a dozen Hurricanes was brought forward, and the fighters eventually shipped in February 1940. Only 11 arrived, however, and by the time they had been assembled the weight of the Russian army and air force had taken its toll on the Finnish air force. The Winter War came to an end on 13 March 1940.

The 11 Hurricanes did enter service, however, despite no spares being available, and the majority went on to see action in the Continuation War against the Soviets (1941–44). Employed as interceptors, the Hurricanes were very popular with the Finnish pilots, who rated them very highly until they began receiving Bf 109s. The Hurricanes shot down several Soviet aircraft during the Continuation War, without loss.

NORWAY

One RAF Hurricane unit, along with No. 263 Squadron's Gladiators, saw action over Norway during May 1940. Number 46 Squadron, under the command of Squadron Leader K. B. B. Cross, was embarked via lighter aboard HMS *Glorious* at Greenock on 10 May. After the ship had crossed the North Sea, the aircraft took off and landed at Skånland and Bardufoss on 25 May; this was the first time a Hurricane had been flown from a carrier.

It was decided that the Gladiators would operate from Skånland and the Hurricanes from Bardufoss. After familiarising themselves with the area around Narvik over the following days, the No. 46 Squadron

OPPOSITE HC-452, now restored and exhibited in the Aviation Museum of Central Finland, shown here at in summer 1942 at Tiiksjarvi airfield, camouflaged from Soviet aircraft by tree branches. (John Dibbs)

ENGAGING THE ENEMY

Like the Spitfire I/II, the Hurricane I was fitted with a Barr & Stroud GM 2 reflector gunsight as standard. This unit, devised by the Barr & Stroud company in 1935, featured a lens through which a large circular graticule was projected onto a circular glass reflector screen 76mm in diameter. The graticule was bisected by a cross, the horizontal bar of which was broken in the centre, with the range/base setting being determined using two knurled rings with their own scale that turned a perspex pointer to various range settings, and an adjustable ring which turned an indicator to indicate wingspan in feet. The internal mechanism then set the gap according to the required range. A central dot was added as a further aiming point. The pilot first set the span dial to the known wingspan of his prospective target, then the range dial to the maximum for accurate fire. When the target coincided with the gap it was within range. The radius of the graticule ring gave the deflection allowance for hitting a target crossing at 100mph. The gunsight was illuminated by a halfsilvered 12-volt lamp in a quick-release holder at the base of the sight body.

A substantial rubber pad was fitted to protect the pilot from injury in the event of a rough landing. Chosen by the RAF as its standard fixed gunsight, the GM 2 was known as the Reflector Sight Mk II in frontline service. The sight was patented in 1937, and the first examples of an initial order of 1,600 reached service squadrons in 1938. The GM 2 sight was used in most British fighters serving with both the RAF and the Fleet Air Arm between 1938 and 1943.

(Jim Laurier © Osprey Publishing)

pilots' first encounter with the enemy came on 28 May. Flying Officers J. W. Lydall in L1806 and P. R. McGregor in L1853 intercepted a Junkers Ju 88 attempting to attack the port and shot it down over Tjelbotn. During the evening, No. 46 Squadron caught a pair of Do 26s preparing to disembark 20 German alpine troops in the Rombaksfjord. Both were shot down, although one managed to carry out a forced landing, after which the crew and ten troops were captured.

By 3 June, it was clear that the British could hold Narvik no longer and a withdrawal began, protected from above by the constant patrols of No. 46 Squadron and its FAA counterparts. By 7 June, the Luftwaffe's position had become much stronger and raids on Narvik increased. During the day, No. 46 Squadron's pilots found themselves defending against three heavy He 111 attacks. That evening Squadron Leader Cross was ordered to destroy all remaining Hurricanes and equipment, and make for a ship in the harbour.

After much negotiation, he managed to convince his senior commanders that he should be allowed to fly his remaining ten Hurricanes onto HMS *Glorious*, despite the fact that neither he nor any of his pilots had landed on a carrier before. Between 1800hrs on 7 June and 0045hrs on 8 June, all ten Hurricanes were landed safely aboard, while the remaining pilots and ground crew headed for Narvik to board MV *Arandora Star* and make for home.

In an effort to distance itself from the danger of a land-based aerial attack, however, *Glorious* inadvertently sailed within range of the German battlecruisers *Scharnhorst* and *Gneisenau*. Despite the valiant efforts of its two supporting destroyers, the ship succumbed to enemy fire and sank at 1740hrs, within 20 minutes of the order to abandon ship being given. Only 40 men survived, including No. 46 Squadron's CO, Squadron Leader Cross, and one pilot, Flight Lieutenant P. G. Jameson; 1,515 seamen and airmen perished.

THE BATTLE OF FRANCE

On 10 May 1940 the German army had begun to push west, heading through the Netherlands, Belgium and Luxembourg, and on into France. The German plan was simple: attack north of the Maginot Line and push through to the English Channel, leaving the BEF separated from the French army. A final push south towards Paris would bring about a swift end to the operation.

By this time some of the Hurricane squadrons in France had relocated, including No. 1 Squadron, which moved from Vassincourt to Berry-au-Bac on the day of the German mobilisation. Number 73 Squadron moved to Reims/Champagne and No. 85 Squadron remained at Lille/Seclin, while No. 87 Squadron moved to Senon. Numbers 607 Squadron at Vitry-en-Artois and 615 Squadron at Abbeville were still flying Gladiators, but were in the process of re-equipping with Hurricanes. These six squadrons had a total

OPPOSITE Hurricane Mk I, L2045 'SD-A', of No. 501 Squadron, loaded onto a railway wagon, awaits transportation along with four Rolls-Royce Merlin engines, during the final evacuation from France. (© IWM C 1674)

strength of 96 of the fighters. As news of the unfolding events reached London, Dowding, as promised, sent three more Hurricane units – Nos. 3, 79 and 504 Squadrons – to bolster the Air Component and No. 501 Squadron to reinforce the AASF.

The ten Hurricane squadrons fought hard from the outset. Number 501 Squadron, which had lost three pilots killed and six more injured when its transport aircraft crashed at Béheniville, still managed to claim 18 enemy aircraft destroyed in the first two days of the fighting, at the expense of two pilots and three aircraft.

Number 87 Squadron was briefly excused escort duty on 11 May, to attack two large formations of Ju 87s over Brussels and Tongres. By the engagement's end, ten enemy aircraft had been shot down for the loss of two pilots and their aircraft. Other early successes included one for No. 3 Squadron, which shot down eight enemy aircraft without loss on 12 May.

The Air Component units had suffered the brunt of RAF losses, in particular Nos. 85 and 87 Squadrons. The former shot down 29 German aircraft during the first nine days of the enemy attack, losing six aircraft and their pilots while no reinforcements made it to the unit's airfield at Merville, where it remained throughout the period. A brief attempt was made to fly Nos. 85 and 87 Squadrons as a combined unit, the latter also suffering heavy losses, but instead both were ordered to return to Britain. Number 85 Squadron left on 22 May and No. 87 Squadron on the 24th.

Dowding was by now under even more pressure to send extra fighters to the aid of France. However, once he explained that a third of his home defence strength had already been expended, the pressure eased from his side of the Channel. It was now time to help the BEF leave France, an exercise that would cost Dowding further valuable pilots and their machines.

DUNKIRK

Preparations for the evacuation of the BEF, under the code name Operation *Dynamo*, had been in the planning since 19 May. The commander of the Air Component had already withdrawn his HQ across the

Channel to Hawkinge, where Air Vice-Marshal (AVM) C. H. B. Blount worked closely with 11 Group's AOC, AVM K. Park, to organise fighter cover over the beaches.

On 26 May the evacuation began, by which time all RAF squadrons had been withdrawn from the Pas-de-Calais. The Hurricane units, on average, only managed to come back with half their original strength, and at Merville alone approximately 20 fighters were left to burn. Both Nos. 607 and 615 Squadrons' Hurricanes were transferred to fully operational units and they returned to Britain with the majority of their original Gladiators. Numbers 213 and 601 Squadrons, which had sent detachments to Merville on 17 May, also managed to return to Britain with their original strength.

All fighter operations over France were now controlled by 11 Group, which could also call up several Spitfire and Defiant squadrons in support of *Dynamo*. The Hurricanes were in action from 20 May, when all Kent-based squadrons were instructed to attack German columns on the Cambrai–Arras road. To keep the pressure on, the aircraft were quickly turned around on any French airfield that had not been overrun.

The BEF's impression, however, was that the RAF had virtually abandoned it. Despite this, German commanders were reporting that the British fighter pilots had achieved air superiority over the Pas-de-Calais for the first time since 10 May.

On the first day of full Dunkirk operations, Park wisely only employed one squadron of fighters over the beachhead at any time while he worked out how Luftwaffe tactics would evolve. One Hurricane and one Spitfire squadron were held at full readiness during daylight hours as well. In contrast, the Luftwaffe could call upon 220 bombers, 60 Bf 110s and a Gruppe of Bf 109Es. Within 48 hours, these numbers were raised by a further 120 Ju 87s and almost as many Bf 109s.

From 29 May, Park increased the number of patrolling fighter squadrons to four in an effort to improve the odds, which had at one point been as high as ten to one in favour of the Luftwaffe. Number 111 Squadron joined the fight during the day, which ended with another 22 enemy aircraft shot down (15 claimed by No. 264 Squadron's Defiants). Four Hurricanes were lost and several limped back to Kent with battle damage.

By 30 May, poor weather had helped the evacuation recover 140,000 men, and the momentum continued through the following day as the Ju 87s remained grounded owing to the bad conditions. However, 1 June was a different story, as a large formation of Ju 87s managed to reach the beachhead between RAF patrols, sinking three destroyers loaded with troops.

The air war continued through 2/3 June, by which time the evacuation was proceeding mainly during darkness to keep casualties to a minimum. The last major enemy bomber raid during *Dynamo* took place on 2 June, when 120 German bombers encountered five Hurricane and Spitfire squadrons over Dunkirk. The RAF pilots not only managed to shoot several of them down, but also prevented them from bombing ships loading troops in the port. Smaller Ju 87 and Ju 88 raids still managed to slip through the RAF fighter screen, but by 3/4 June the last of 328,226 British and French troops had been evacuated.

During the nine days of Operation *Dynamo*, the RAF had suffered heavy losses, with 84 pilots missing or killed and 135 Hurricanes, Spitfires, Blenheims and Defiants lost. But this was not the end for the AASF's Hurricane and Battle pilots. It had been split from the main BEF and was now withdrawing westwards across France. While a few Hurricanes continued to provide air cover for the retreating Allied troops, they were bolstered by Nos. 17 and 242 Squadrons, sent to Le Mans from 8 to 16 June before withdrawing to Jersey and Guernsey.

The final Hurricane units to leave France were Nos. 1, 73 and 501 Squadrons. Number 1 Squadron was evacuated via St Nazaire on 18 June, while No. 73 Squadron's remaining aircraft were burned at Nantes and it left France via St Malo on 17 June. Number 501 Squadron's final role was to cover the evacuation of troops from Cherbourg on 19 June and it returned with eight Hurricanes to mainland Britain, via Jersey, the following day.

The Battle of France was over and Britain braced itself for the next onslaught. The campaign had cost the RAF 949 aircraft; 477 of these were fighters and 386 of those were Hurricanes, the type having taken on the majority of the aerial fighting.

MALTA – THE BEGINNING

The Hurricane began a long and crucial association with the isolated yet strategically important island of Malta from early August 1940. Responsibility for the island's defence fell upon the shoulders of Squadron Leader D. W. Balden, leading No. 261 Squadron. The unit included two components, the Fighter Flight, already established on Malta with the Sea Gladiator, and 418 Flight, originally formed at Abbotsinch with a dozen Hurricanes. The latter embarked in HMS *Argus*, bound for the Mediterranean, and then flew from the carrier on 2 August to relieve the hard-pressed Gladiators and a few Hurricanes that had already arrived on Malta from Britain, via France and North Africa. That same day, the two flights were amalgamated at Luqa to become No. 261 Squadron.

Initially, the attacking Corpo Aereo Italiano (Italian Air Force) confidently despatched unescorted SM.79 bombers, but once the Gladiators began shooting them down they were withdrawn and replaced by fighter sweeps, in an attempt to wipe out the RAF defenders. By now, however, the first Hurricanes to operate in the Mediterranean theatre had become operational and it was not long before they were making their mark against the Italians and the Luftwaffe.

The aerial bombardment eased until November 1940, when the Axis embarked upon a high-level bombing campaign against Valletta and Luqa, followed by fighter-bomber raids. These were dealt with by positioning the Hurricanes at high altitude and the squadron's Gladiators lower down. On 9 January 1941, 12 Macchi MC.200s carried out a fighter-bomber raid, but only eight managed to escape following a mauling by No. 261 Squadron.

The Luftwaffe mounted its own concentrated campaign between 16 and 19 January, No. 261 Squadron claiming 40 aircraft destroyed, five probables and 12 damaged. During March and April 1941, a further 35 enemy machines were destroyed, with four probables and 21 damaged, at the expense of three pilots and seven Hurricanes.

In May 1941, No. 261 Squadron was disbanded at Ta Kali, its personnel and aircraft transferring to No. 185 Squadron.

THE BATTLE OF BRITAIN

Following the evacuation at Dunkirk, France held out for another fortnight, giving Dowding valuable time to regroup his forces, and all his fighter squadrons were back on British soil by 1 July 1940. Of the 58 operational squadrons available to Fighter Command that day, 29 were flying the Hurricane, equipped with 347 'combat

ready' aircraft, and 115 that were unserviceable but likely to be flying again within a few days.

Some 527 pilots were available to fly the Hurricanes, although not all were classed 'checked out fully on type', giving the Hawker greater availability compared to the Spitfire, Blenheim and Defiant squadrons. This dominance was no more evident than in Park's strategically vital 11 Group, which was responsible for protecting the south-east of England.

The initial Luftwaffe forays came early in July 1940, at first confined to high-level reconnaissance sorties by single aircraft, followed by a few organised Ju 87 attacks on merchant shipping in the Channel. It soon became apparent that these probing raids were designed to give the Luftwaffe crews experience of 'over-sea' operations, which they had not been trained for, and to draw out RAF fighters to engage on needless and often wasteful patrols.

The tactic was confirmed on 7 July, when the Hurricanes of No. 145 Squadron, under the command of Squadron Leader J. R. A. Peel, began a standing

patrol over a convoy off the Isle of Wight. During the morning, Peel and Pilot Officer E. Wakeham shot down a Do 17P before handing over the patrol to No. 43 Squadron, which also shot down a Dornier that ultimately crashed in France. Squadron Leader M. Aitken of No. 601 Squadron claimed a third Dornier before the day was out.

However, in an attempt to catch the RAF unawares, the Luftwaffe despatched several Staffeln of Bf 109Es to attack the Hurricanes and Spitfires coming and going from their patrols. Numbers 54 and 65

OPPOSITE At 0745hrs on 15 May 1940, a large formation of Bf 110Cs (possibly from I./ZG 26) overflew Berry-au-Bac airfield at 15,000ft. They formed part of the escort for bombers sent to attack Laon. Six Hurricane Is from No. 1 Squadron's 'B' Flight were scrambled, with Flight Lieutenant Peter Prosser Hanks leading the chase in N2380. Hanks later recalled: 'We got above them and I dived vertically on the leader and fired a burst, allowing deflection, and he just blew up. Nothing left of him but a few small pieces.' Hanks shot down a second Bf 110 moments later, but his own fighter was badly hit and he was forced to bail out of the blazing aircraft. (Gareth Hector © Osprey Publishing)

Squadrons' Spitfires bore the brunt of the assault, losing five aircraft between them. A single Hurricane loss, believed to have been Hurricane Mk I P2756, flown by Squadron Leader J. D. C. Joslin of No. 79 Squadron, is thought to have been the result of an attack by several Spitfires. Joslin bailed out of his burning Hurricane over Chilverton Elms, Kent, but did not survive. Three days later, No. 79 Squadron, which had been in action for two months without a break, was withdrawn to Turnhouse for a rest.

The largest dogfight so far to involve the Hurricane took place on 10 July, the first day of the Battle of Britain. Twenty-two Hurricanes from Nos. 32, 56 and 111 Squadrons, along with eight Spitfires from No. 74 Squadron, attacked 26 Do 17 and Do 215 bombers, 30 Bf 110s and 20 Bf 109Es over a convoy off the Kent coast.

For No. 111 Squadron, led by Squadron Leader J. M. Thompson, it was the first time it had used the line abreast, head-on style of bomber attack. Flying Officer T. P. K. Higgs collided with a 3./KG 2 Dornier during the first attack and was forced to bail out of crippled Hurricane Mk I P3671, only to drown in the Channel. By the end of the encounter, two Dorniers, six Bf 110s and a Bf 109 had been destroyed, four other bombers damaged and several fighters claimed as probables.

Hurricanes were also involved in an action on 19 July that exposed the inadequacies of the Defiant as a 'convoy escort' fighter. Number 264 Squadron, which had been moved south from Turnhouse to replace No. 79 Squadron, was bounced by ten Bf 109Es, and within the space of a minute, five of the nine Defiants were spiralling down in flames. If it had not been for the arrival and prompt action of No. 111 Squadron, the remaining four would have joined their squadron mates in the sea.

By the end of July, the Luftwaffe had yet to attempt a major bombing raid beyond the extreme southern counties. In terms of victories achieved, it was still the Hurricane, by a whisker, that led the tally board. By 31 July, Hurricane claims were 87 enemy aircraft compared to the Spitfire's 71, comprising 17 He 111s, 15 Do 17s, 14 Bf 110s, 12 Bf 109s, ten Ju 87s and seven Ju 88s, plus 12 'other aircraft'. On the opposite side of the coin, the Luftwaffe had claimed 40 Hurricanes shot down, although at least two of these had actually been victims of friendly fire.

The Luftwaffe carried out another large raid on the morning of 13 August, a day when Fighter Command could boast 678 aircraft, 353 of them Hurricanes. The main Luftwaffe success of the day came when an unescorted raid by 74 KG 2 Dorniers bombed the airfield at Eastchurch, although five of their number were shot down by Hurricanes. Flight Lieutenant R. L. Smith of No. 151 Squadron claimed one of the Dorniers flying L1750, an experimental Hurricane armed with a pair of 20mm cannon. He opened fire at 300yds, causing one bomber to burst into flames and leaving another trailing smoke.

On 16 August, No. 249 Squadron, along with several Hurricane squadrons, was destined to see a

OPPOSITE A Hurricane on the tail of a German bomber, November 1939. (Photo by adoc-photos/Corbis via Getty Images)

great deal of action. Another 16 bombers, nine dive bombers, eight Bf 110s and 17 Bf 109s were shot down, 19 of them falling to the guns of Hurricanes. Flight Lieutenant E. J. B. Nicolson led one of the day's patrols in No. 249 Squadron Hurricane Mk I L3576. He was leading a flight of three Hurricanes when he spotted the beginnings of a bombing raid on Gosport and just as his fighters positioned themselves for an attack, several Bf 109s bounced them.

Nicolson's aircraft and that of his wingman, Pilot Officer M. A. King, were set alight. Meanwhile, Nicolson had spotted a Bf 110 and doggedly remained focused on his quarry, riddling it with gunfire, before bailing out with serious burns to his hands and face. King had already been forced to bail out and as the two airmen floated down they came under fire from a group of Local Defence Volunteers (later known as the Home Guard), who mistook them for Germans.

King is believed to have been dead before he hit the ground. Nicolson suffered a shotgun wound to the buttock, in addition to his already serious injuries. Following a lengthy stay in hospital, he was awarded the Victoria Cross for his determination against the enemy, the only such award presented to a Fighter Command pilot.

Poor weather on 27 August gave some respite to aircrew on both sides of the Channel, but approximately 100 Luftflotte 2 Dorniers set course up the Thames Estuary the following day. It looked as if the large enemy formation was about to attack the airfields at Hornchurch and North Weald, but instead it split into two and bombed Rochford and Eastchurch. As the Hurricanes of No. 56 Squadron from North Weald tore into the bombers, a large wave of Bf 109s joined the fray; the Spitfires of No. 603 Squadron from Hornchurch initially took them on. After another frantic battle, nine enemy aircraft had been shot down,

OPPOSITE A group of pilots of No. 303 Polish Squadron, RAF at Leconfield in November 1940. All except two of these pilots achieved ace status. (Photo by S A Devon/IWM via Getty Images)

but No. 603 Squadron had lost four aircraft and No. 56 Squadron three, although two of its pilots turned up safe and one was wounded. It had been a light day for Hurricane losses, with just four downed, while the Luftwaffe had lost a total of 28 by the day's end.

As the fighter-versus-fighter loss rate remained static, by 30 August Park was ordering his controllers not to expose his forces in free chasing combats with Bf 109s. The Hurricanes of Nos. 1, 56 and 242 Squadrons were unleashed against a large enemy raid north of London after their fighter escort was forced to turn back for France. Thirteen Fighter Command squadrons were in action against the raid of approximately 300 aircraft, which attacked targets from Harwich to Oxford in groups of 10 to 20 aircraft. Twenty-nine enemy aircraft were shot down, and from the three Hurricane squadrons engaged, No. 56 Squadron lost two aircraft, with one pilot injured and the other safe. 'A' Flight of No. 253 Squadron, led by Squadron Leader T. Gleave, was less fortunate when it broke cloud during a climb only to find itself in the middle of a formation of approximately 90 Bf 109s. Gleave instinctively attacked and within a minute had shot down three Bf 109s and probably a fourth before making his escape. His three wingmen were not so lucky, all being shot down; two were killed and the third injured.

The week beginning Saturday 31 August was by far the most critical week of the Battle of Britain. It saw 55 pilots killed and 78 wounded, and the loss of 107 Hurricanes and 71 Spitfires in combat. This rate of attrition represented an entire squadron of pilots being lost every day plus almost two squadrons' worth of aircraft. Units were now being withdrawn to rest at a moment's notice, to be replaced by fresh squadrons from the north of England and Scotland. Very often

OPPOSITE Flight Lieutenant Ian 'Widge' Gleed downs the first of two Bf 110Cs from III./ZG 76 to fall to his guns off Portland Bill during the bitter fighting of 15 August 1940. Gleed was flying his assigned Hurricane I (P2798) on this occasion, and he used it to down ten German aircraft – including six Bf 110s – between 18 May and 30 September, 1940. (Gareth Hector © Osprey Publishing)

the squadron being withdrawn only had four or five serviceable aircraft on strength, and such was the extent of the losses that they were temporarily reduced to little more than training units.

Some of the older Hurricane squadrons, all of them eager to see action again, were now brought back into battle. Saturday 31 August was by far the worst day for the Hurricane squadrons. Numbers 56 and 79 Squadrons each lost four fighters, No. 1 (RCAF) and 601 Squadrons lost three apiece, and Nos. 85, 151, 253, 257 and 310 Squadrons each lost two, while Nos. 1, 111, and 501 Squadrons each suffered the loss of a single Hurricane. It had been a truly horrendous day.

Among the pilot casualties, three were squadron commanders. A Bf 110 shot No. 85 Squadron's Squadron Leader P. W. Townsend down over Tunbridge, but he managed to bail out with a wounded foot. A Ju 88 shot No. 253 Squadron's outgoing commanding officer down over Cudham and his nominated replacement, Squadron Leader H. M. Starr, was also unlucky. Fighters shot his Hurricane, L1830, down over Grove Ferry and he was killed.

The weather window in which the German invasion was planned to occur was rapidly closing by mid-September, but this did not stop the Luftwaffe commander, Hermann Göring, from giving it his all again on 15 September. However, the Luftwaffe found itself up against a revitalised RAF, which managed to launch 336 fighter sorties and by the end of the day's fighting, 21 enemy aircraft had been destroyed; Fighter Command was far from defeated. Hitler was forced to shelve his plans to invade Britain.

From this point, the momentum of the Luftwaffe raids began to falter until 27 September, when three major attacks were despatched from France between 0900hrs and 1530hrs by approximately 640 enemy aircraft. All three raids targeted London, but many of the formations

OPPOSITE Squadron Leader Douglas Bader DSO (front centre) with some of the pilots of No. 242 (Canadian) Squadron, grouped around his Hurricane at Duxford, September 1940. (Photo by S A Devon/IWM via Getty Images)

were broken up by determined head-on Hurricane attacks, while the Spitfires fought furiously with the Bf 109 escorts. By the early evening, another 131 enemy aircraft lay strewn across the English countryside at a cost of 30 fighters, 13 of them Hurricanes.

The last great success of the Hurricane during the final stages of the Battle of Britain was against the Corpo Aereo Italiano. On 11 November, the same day the Fleet Air Arm carried out its successful Taranto attack, the Hurricanes of Nos. 17, 46 and 257 Squadrons intercepted a force of ten BR.20s escorted by 40 CR.42s, G.50s and a few Bf 109Es, intent on bombing Harwich.

Under the temporary command of Flight Lieutenant H. P. 'Cowboy' Blatchford, No. 257 Squadron claimed nine Italian aircraft and a single Bf 109E. After Blatchford had run out of ammunition, he attacked a CR.42 by ramming it and 'milling the enemy's top wing with his propeller'. No Hurricanes were lost, the Italians never returned to Britain in daylight, and by the end of 1940 they had been withdrawn from their Belgian bases.

Fighter Command had clearly defeated the Luftwaffe, but the Battle of France and Battle of Britain had taken their toll, with more than 50 per cent of the highly experienced pre-war pilots killed. New leaders, including Douglas Bader, Bob Stanford Tuck, Roland Beamont and James Harry 'Ginger' Lacey, to name a few, would help carry Fighter Command through its most difficult period, however, as it changed role from defensive to offensive in a matter of months.

Conjecture remains as to the exact Battle of Britain statistics, but Fighter Command claimed 2,741 enemy kills, 55 per cent by Hurricanes, 42 per cent by Spitfires and 3 per cent other types. Airmen whose countries had been overrun by the Germans scored many of these kills, including Czech pilot Sergeant Josef Frantisek of No. 303 (Polish) Squadron, who became the highest

OPPOSITE Flying Officer V. C. Woodward of 'B' Flight, No. 33 Squadron, dons his parachute beside his Hurricane Mk I, at Fuka, Egypt. Woodward had shot down six enemy aircraft, and was to gain a further 19 victories before he left the Middle East theatre in September 1941. (© IWM ME(RAF) 167)

scorer with 17 kills; he was lost in Hurricane Mk I R4175 at Ewell, Surrey on 8 October 1940.

ON THE BACK FOOT

When Italy declared war on Britain in June 1940, only one Hurricane was available to the RAF in the Middle East. Several more were making their way south across France, however, arriving at Sidi Barrani, Egypt to equip a flight of No. 80 Squadron under the command of Squadron Leader R. C. Jonas, whose main aircraft was the Gladiator. As more aircraft followed, No. 274 Squadron was re-formed at Amiriya on 19 August from elements of Nos. 33, 80 and 112 Squadrons to become the first all-Hurricane unit in the Middle East. With the exception of the odd encounter with a few SM.79s, the Hurricane saw very little action until the first major Libyan campaign began in December 1940.

When the campaign began, Nos. 33 and 274 Squadrons were already operational, and No. 73 Squadron joined them to bolster in-theatre fighter strength following an epic flight across West Africa after taking off from HMS *Furious*. From January 1941, encounters with German aircraft were on the increase, especially with Bf 109Es, which were considerably more challenging than their Italian counterparts.

In February 1941, the British advance across the desert petered out. At the same time, several additional Hurricanes were placed on No. 80 Squadron's strength following its departure to Greece, where it had been struggling on with the Gladiator. Number 33 Squadron bolstered No. 80 Squadron during the month, moving to Eleusis and then Larissa.

March saw Rommel's Afrika Korps push the British back into Egypt. At the same time, No. 274 Squadron was withdrawn from action for a rest, leaving only the Hurricanes of Nos. 73 Squadron and 3 (Royal Australian Air Force (RAAF)) Squadron to face the Luftwaffe. Number 6 Squadron was also in theatre, but its Hurricanes were TacR variants and not all were armed. In opposition were the Bf 109Es of the highly experienced I./Jagdgeschwader (JG) 27, with the likes of Leutnant Hans-Joachim Marseille and

Oberfeldwebel O. Schultz, and the Bf 110Cs of the equally experienced III./Zerstörergeschwader (ZG) 26. Both units inflicted heavy losses upon the less experienced Hurricane pilots.

In Greece, the German forces began their offensive in April 1941 and despite a spirited defence, the Allies were pushed out very quickly. After withdrawing to Crete, the remnants of Nos. 33, 80 and 112 Squadrons continued the fight until the last aircraft fell. But it was in Greek skies that the officer commanding (OC) No. 33 Squadron, Squadron Leader M. T. St J. 'Pat' Pattle DFC, became the RAF's unofficial highest scorer of World War II, with at least 50 victories. Of these, 26 were over Italian aircraft, 15 while Pattle was flying the Gladiator and the remainder in the Hurricane, making him the highest scoring pilot on both types.

Elsewhere, the Hurricane was faring better. The three South African Air Force (SAAF) squadrons flying the type over East Africa had gained complete superiority over the Italian Air Force. Number 2 (SAAF) Squadron, flying Gladiators, Hurricanes and even a few Furies, covered southern Ethiopia, bolstered later by Hurricanes from No. 3 (SAAF) Squadron. Further north, the Gladiators of No. 1 (SAAF) Squadron covered the skies over Eritrea, until Hurricanes replaced them from December 1940.

By April 1941, Commonwealth troops had overwhelmed the Italian ground forces, and Eritrea and the Ethiopian capital were in Allied hands. The bulk of the Italian forces surrendered in May, although their remnants held out until November; throughout this period there was no aerial opposition for the SAAF Hurricanes to combat.

ACROSS THE CHANNEL

Early 1941 saw the introduction of the Hurricane Mk IIB, with Nos. 601 (County of London) and 605 (County of Warwick) Squadrons, followed by the first Mk IICs with Nos. 1 and 3 Squadrons. These units launched offensive operations over Northern Europe, which, although often costly, showed that the RAF was finally fighting back, rather than merely defending.

During 1941, 13 squadrons re-equipped with the Hurricane, but by year's end, 25 Hurricane squadrons had themselves been re-equipped, 19 of them with Spitfires. In October the Hurricane began fighter-bomber operations, proving particularly effective against shipping and coastal targets. Using the cannon-armed Mk IIC, Nos. 1 and 3 Squadrons achieved great success on night intruder operations and continued to do so well into 1942.

Early 1942 saw even more squadrons giving up their Hurricanes for Spitfires and Typhoons. Many new units were supplied with Hurricanes before they became operational, more often than not replacing them with a modern counterpart. There was an exception, however, when No. 184 Squadron formed at Colerne on 1 December 1942 with the potent Hurricane Mk IID.

The last major action from British bases to involve the Hurricane was Operation *Jubilee*, the raid on Dieppe on 19 August 1942. Eight Hurricane units took part in the ill-fated operation, Nos. 3, 32, 43, 87, 174, 175, 245 and 253 Squadrons. All suffered casualties, totalling 12 pilots killed and 27 aircraft lost.

The formation of the 2nd Tactical Air Force (2TAF) in June 1943 marked an unexpected resurgence in demand for the Hurricane fighter-bomber, thanks to the general unavailability of its replacement, the Typhoon. The Hurricane Mk IV was the weapon of choice and Nos. 137, 164, 184, 186 and 438 Squadrons all filled an important gap in 2TAF's ground attack capability during 1943. Number 184 Squadron, operating from Manston in Kent, gained the honour of being the first Hurricane unit to successfully carry out a rocket attack against enemy shipping, on 29 July. Numbers 137 and 164 Squadrons also became masters of the art of maritime rocket attacks, but by the beginning of 1944 the Hurricane was finally superseded by the Typhoon.

OPPOSITE Six Hurricane Mk IIBs of 'B' Flight, No. 601 Squadron based at Duxford, Cambridgeshire, flying in starboard echelon formation near Thaxted, Essex, 21 August 1941. (Photo by B J Daventry/IWM via Getty Images)

In British skies, only No. 309 Squadron, operating from Snailwell in Cambridgeshire and then Drem from April 1944, was left flying any mark of Hurricane in an operational capacity. It received the Mk IV in February, followed by the Mk IIC in April, using both in the air defence of Scotland until October 1944, when Mustang Mk IIIs replaced the Hawkers.

CONVOY PROTECTION

Even as the RAF moved onto offensive operations over the Continent, Britain faced a threat that placed its continued existence in the balance. Hitler's Germany was mounting a concerted, sustained effort to destroy ships bringing essential supplies of food and arms to British shores, especially from North America, but also North Africa and other regions. Soon, convoys would also be plying routes between Great Britain and Soviet Russia and these too would be subject to vicious harassment.

Desperately short of conventional carriers, the Royal Navy equipped five vessels as Fighter Catapult

Ships. Equipped with the Fairey Fulmar they gained no success, but soon the Sea Hurricane Mk IA was available and on 2 August 1941, Lieutenant Commander R. W. H. Everett scored the first kill for an FCS and a Sea Hurricane, downing an Fw 200 harassing a convoy sailing from North Africa.

The FCS and civilian CAM-ships continued providing essential convoy protection until July 1943, latterly joining the routes to Gibraltar. They had proven the value of organic airpower and paved the way for escort carrier operations just as soon as such ships could be delivered from the US yards. And when the escort carriers were commissioned, their complements typically included Sea Hurricanes or Grumman Martlets as their fighter equipment.

Running battles between convoys, their escorts and enemy submarines and aircraft were common, but few so dramatic as that surrounding convoy PQ18, which sailed from Scotland on 3 September 1942, bound for Murmansk. Its predecessor, PQ17, had departed Iceland for Russia on 27 June and, lacking air cover,

made it through with only 10 of its 33 ships afloat. Less than a week after its departure, PQ18 rendezvoused with HMS *Avenger* off Iceland, armed with 12 Sea Hurricane Mk IB fighters.

Enemy aircraft again took a heavy toll, attacking relentlessly between 13 and 18 September, but 26 out of 39 merchantmen made it through, while the Luftwaffe lost 41 aircraft, most of them to the Sea Hurricanes. Four of the latter fell, with three pilots rescued, although the convoy's own protective fire had accidentally accounted for three of the fighters. While PQ18 perhaps exemplified the Sea Hurricane's success on convoy escort duties, it was not its most important foray in the role. That had come a month earlier, with Operation *Pedestal*, a vital resupply of Malta.

OPPOSITE Sea Hurricane Mark I, V6733, of the Merchant Ship Fighter Unit, on the fo'c'sle catapult on board CAM ship SS *Empire Darwin*, in a convoy heading for North Africa. Note the flaps pre-selected in the take-off position. (Photo by Sgt C J Dawson/IWM via Getty Images)

DEFENCE OF MALTA

Malta gained its Hurricane unit on 12 May 1941, when No. 185 Squadron was re-formed at Hal Far from the remains of No. 261 Squadron and 1430 Flight, both of which had been defending the island since August 1940. Another Hurricane unit, No. 46 Squadron, which was only meant to be transiting through Malta on 20 May en route to Egypt, was retained on the island. Most of its strength eventually continued to Egypt, but No. 46 Squadron left its pilots behind to form the nucleus of No. 126 Squadron, which was re-formed at Ta Kali on 28 June 1941. The day after No. 46 Squadron's arrival, another Hurricane unit, No. 249 Squadron, landed on Malta via HMS *Furious* and *Ark Royal* to bolster the precious island's defences. During late 1941, the well-equipped Luftwaffe instigated its second attempt to wipe Malta off the map. Further reinforcement with the arrival of Nos. 242 and 605 Squadrons was welcome, but the Hurricane was beginning to show its age against the enemy fighters, particularly the Bf 109F.

The first of many Spitfires to arrive in the Mediterranean was despatched to Malta in the spring of 1942. Number 126 Squadron re-equipped first with the Spitfire in March, followed by Nos. 185 and 249 Squadrons in May. The Hurricanes of No. 229 Squadron moved to the island on 29 March, but just over a month later the unit disbanded at Hal Far to re-form at Ta Kali four months later with Spitfires.

But the Sea Hurricane had one more crucial contribution to make in Malta's fight for survival. Operational *Pedestal* surrounded a convoy that simply had to make it to the island; if it did not, Malta would run out of fuel in September. On 11/12 August, *Pedestal's* 13 merchant ships and SS *Ohio*, a tanker laden with 12,000 tons of fuel oil, passed into the Mediterranean. A powerful Royal Navy force of 36 warships sailed in parallel, including two battleships and the aircraft carriers HMS *Eagle*, *Indomitable* and *Victorious*.

Between them, the carriers embarked 72 fighters, comprising Fulmars, Martlets and 39 Sea Hurricanes. *Eagle* went down early in the battle, while Ju 87s made it through the fighters to hit *Indomitable* hard, taking it out of the fight. The surviving aircraft now operated off *Victorious*, although 16 had gone down with *Eagle* and 13 more were lost in combat. The remainder fought on through the 14th, protecting a convoy that was now down to two merchant ships and the tanker, all of which made it into Valetta harbour on the 15th. Malta had effectively been saved and the Sea Hurricane had been a vital tool in its salvation. The Hurricane had done its duty for Malta; it was not seen on the island operationally again.

AIR DEFENCE IN RUSSIA

After Hitler turned his attention away from Britain, he began his campaign to invade Russia, under Operation *Barbarossa*. The German Blitzkrieg tactics initially overwhelmed the giant country, which lost

OPPOSITE A Hurricane Mk IIB, Z5253 'GA-25' of No. 134 Squadron taxies out past Russian sentries at Vaenga, October 1941. (Photo by Royal Air Force Official Photographer/IWM via Getty Images)

much of its air force on the ground through persistent Luftwaffe raids.

Britain came to Russia's aid by despatching two Hurricane Mk IIB units, Nos. 81 and 134 Squadrons, under the control of 151 Wing, which arrived at Vaenga in HMS *Argus* on 7 September 1941. The main objective of 151 Wing was to train Russian pilots in the art of flying the Hurricane, which would at first be specifically used for the defence of Murmansk. However, there were plenty of opportunities to attack the enemy during this 'training' period and before the aircraft were handed over to the Russians, RAF pilots had shot down 16 German aircraft for the loss of one Hurricane. By November, 151 Wing and its squadrons were sailing back to Britain after handing their aircraft over to the 72nd Regiment of the Soviet Naval Fleet.

The Russians later used the Hurricane in the ground attack role, the aircraft being particularly effective against enemy armour when armed with RPs. By the war's end, 2,776 Hurricane Mk IIs had been supplied to Russia.

NORTH AFRICA, THE MEDITERRANEAN AND MIDDLE EAST

The number of Hurricane units in the Middle East continued to increase from May 1941. First to arrive was No. 213 Squadron, followed by No. 238 Squadron in July and No. 229 Squadron in September, all equipped with the Hurricane Mk I. Initially, they were attached to other Hurricane units since they were all understrength, but their arrival was warmly received.

Number 30 Squadron, which originally operated the Blenheim in Greece, was re-equipped with the Hurricane Mk I in June 1941 at Amiriya, while Nos. 33 and 80 Squadrons were brought back on line following their mauling in Crete. The latter found itself in action again as part of Operation *Exporter*, the Allied invasion of Vichy French-controlled Syria and the Lebanon during June and July 1941. Number 260 Squadron joined the fray during the later stages of the operation, flying detachments from Beirut and El Bassa during August.

Number 127 Squadron, re-formed at Habbaniyah in June 1941, also supported the operation, flying

Gladiators and Hurricane Mk Is. Also worthy of mention is No. 806 Squadron, FAA, whose pilots flew ex-RAF Hurricanes during Operation *Exporter* and continued to do so until the end of 1942 as part of the Royal Navy Fighter Squadron in the Western Desert. When the short and very successful operation came to an end, No. 127 Squadron was disbanded and absorbed into No. 261 Squadron, which remained in theatre, providing air cover for Allied forces in Iran.

After the last of the Italian forces surrendered in East Africa, Nos. 1 and 2 (SAAF) Squadrons moved to Iranian airfields. On arrival, No. 2 (SAAF) Squadron converted to the Tomahawk, with No. 3 (SAAF) Squadron not too far behind. By the beginning of the next big offensive in North Africa, Operation *Crusader*, the Western Desert Air Force (WDAF) was 12 Hurricane squadrons lighter. In support of *Crusader*, No. 80 Squadron flew fighter-bomber operations over the desert. However, the Hurricane had become increasingly vulnerable to the newly introduced Bf 109F.

Several Hurricane squadrons, including Nos. 94, 260 and 450, had converted to Kittyhawks by mid-1942, but by the beginning of the battle of El Alamein in October quite a few remained and even more followed. Numbers 127 and 335 (Greek) Squadrons joined the fray over the desert, while No. 40 (SAAF) Squadron arrived to carry out tactical reconnaissance. Number 7 (SAAF) Squadron also moved to the area, only to be absorbed by No. 6 Squadron, flying the Mk IID tank-buster.

During the main battle of El Alamein and the subsequent offensive, General Bernard Montgomery had eight Hurricane fighter-bomber squadrons, which also delivered air defence against Stuka attacks on his troops including the Mk IICs of No. 73 Squadron, which specialised in night strafing attacks; Nos. 208 and 40 (SAAF) Squadron flying TacR operations; and Nos. 94 and 417 (RCAF) Squadrons for area defence.

After Montgomery pushed forward, Nos. 213 and 238 Squadrons had been ordered to fly ahead to a

landing ground out in the desert, far behind German lines. From there, their Hurricanes carried out strafing attacks on enemy troops and vehicles and generally made a nuisance of themselves. These two units, alongside No. 73 Squadron, which continued its night raids, and the reconnaissance No. 40 (SAAF) Squadron, were the only Hurricane outfits to move with the Eighth Army.

Meanwhile, a successful invasion in North Africa would force Germany into fighting on two fronts, and Allied forces began moving for Operation *Torch*, aimed at taking Morocco and Algeria, both under Vichy French control. A massive naval strike force was assembled, including a mixed British/US force of three fleet carriers and seven escort carriers; among the latter, HMS *Avenger*, *Biter* and *Dasher* all embarked Sea Hurricane Mk IICs.

Several RAF Hurricane units were also transferred from Britain in support. The Hurricane Mk IICs of No. 43 Squadron were first to reach the theatre, arriving at Maison Blanche on the day of the invasion, 8 November 1942. Later, Nos. 32, 87, 225, 241 and 253 Squadrons joined them, along with several Spitfire units. After the invasion, several Hurricanes were retained for local defence and convoy patrol duties, but it was not long before Spitfires took these roles over.

Torch was the Sea Hurricane's last major combat outing, with the Seafire, Grumman Hellcat and Vought Corsair rapidly replacing it. Nonetheless, 12 aircraft from *Biter* and *Dasher* downed five Vichy Dewoitine D.520s on 11 November after they had decimated an FAA Fairey Albacore formation. The tables were turned on the 15th, though, when *Avenger* and 14 Sea Hurricanes were lost to a German submarine.

OPPOSITE No. 6 Squadron attacking German armour during the North African campaign. The normal technique was to begin at 5,000ft, dive until reaching a speed of 254mph, and then, with the throttle wide open, to approach the target at between 20 and 40ft above the ground. At 1,000yds, the first of three pairs of 40mm shells were let loose before the aircraft broke away, usually giving the tank very little time to retaliate. (Simon Smith © Osprey Publishing)

As the North African campaign rumbled on, only the Hurricane Mk IIDs of No. 6 Squadron remained as part of Montgomery's armoury on the front line at the beginning of Operation *Pugilist* in mid-March 1943. Once Rommel had been evicted from North Africa in May, several more Hurricane squadrons re-equipped with Spitfires, and during Operation *Husky*, the invasion of Sicily in July 1943, only No. 73 Squadron was still operating Hurricanes over the Allied forces, in its night flying role. Number 6 Squadron was in the process of converting to the Mk IV, while those Hurricane units that remained in North Africa were allocated patrol duties along the North African coast rather than being committed to battle.

When the fighting finally came to an end in May 1945, only Nos. 6 and 351 Squadrons were still equipped with the Hurricane. Number 351 Squadron was transferred to the Yugoslav Air Force on 15 June 1945, while No. 6 Squadron only began withdrawing its trusty Mk IVs in January 1947, becoming, by a large margin, the RAF's last Hurricane squadron.

SINGAPORE, CEYLON AND BURMA

When the Japanese began their bloody campaign in the Far East in December 1941, not a single Hurricane was based in the theatre. At the time, several pilots from Nos. 17, 135, 136 and 232 Squadrons were en route to the Middle East, but were diverted to the Far East. They arrived at Seletar, Singapore on 13 January 1942, where all the pilots flew under the banner of No. 232 Squadron, flying a few Mk IIBs. On 28 January, the rest of No. 232 Squadron arrived, along with the Hurricanes of No. 258 Squadron, both units flying their aircraft off the carrier HMS *Indomitable*.

They remained until Singapore's fall on 15 February 1942. What remained of both squadrons withdrew to Java where they combined with parts of Nos. 242 and 605 Squadrons, which had failed to reach Malta. The rate of attrition was so high that within a matter

OPPOSITE Hurricane Mk IIDs of No. 6 Squadron rolling out at Gabes, Tunisia, soon after noon on 6 April 1943 for a tank-busting raid. (Photo by Royal Air Force Official Photographer/ IWM via Getty Images)

of days only a small part of No. 242 Squadron remained, until it was dispersed at Tasikmalaya on 10 March. The Hurricanes had shot down an untold number of enemy aircraft, but the sheer weight of numbers of the Japanese air and ground forces quickly overwhelmed the token force.

Number 17 Squadron arrived in Mingaladon, Burma on 16 January 1942 and was re-equipped with the Mk IIA. It prepared for the Japanese onslaught alongside the Buffaloes of No. 67 Squadron and P-40s of the American Volunteer Group (AVG). Number 135 Squadron arrived at Mingaladon on 28 January and was re-equipped with the Hurricane Mk IIB. The scene was now set for one of the longest fighting retreats in RAF history.

Both Nos. 17 and 135 Squadrons performed valiantly against the endless flow of enemy aircraft

OPPOSITE Ground crews prepare a Hurribomber at a forward airstrip in Burma as a bullock cart trundles across the airfield, circa 1943. (Photo by Paul Popper/Popperfoto/Getty Images)

until the remains of both were pushed back to India. They suffered considerably more losses from air attack than air-to-air combat, and by March 1942 were down to only a few serviceable Hurricanes. The same month, HMS *Indomitable* delivered two more Hurricane units, Nos. 30 and 261 Squadrons, both arriving at Ratmalana, Ceylon on the 8th. It was also at Ratmalana that the surviving No. 258 Squadron pilots, routed from Java, arrived to re-form the unit with the Hurricane Mk I and Mk IIB.

The three Hurricane and several FAA Fulmar squadrons successfully defended Ceylon from relentless air attack by Admiral Nagumo's carrier striking force between 5 and 9 April 1942. But the battle cost the Royal Navy dearly at sea, and while many attacking aircraft were shot down, the Hurricane squadrons also suffered terrible losses.

With the Japanese tide over Ceylon stemmed, the number of Hurricanes in theatre rapidly rose and by late 1942 there were 13 operational squadrons. Two of these, Nos. 17 and 79 Squadrons, were put to the test in the defence of Calcutta. Operating from Red Road, the two squadrons were augmented by Nos. 67 and 615 Squadrons at Alipore and Jessore, respectively. Once again, despite heaving bombing, the Japanese were kept at bay and after they had stretched themselves as far west as they could go, the first campaign in the Far East to push the enemy back began in Burma from early 1943. However, despite the addition of No. 28 Squadron, which re-equipped with Hurricane Mk IIBs from the Lysander Mk II and made an initial good advance down the Mayun Peninsula, the Allies had been pushed back into India again by May.

More Hurricane squadrons were established in the region during 1943, when Nos. 11, 20 and 60 Squadrons, former Blenheim operators, were re-equipped with the Mk IIB, IIC and IID, the latter proving as useful over the jungle as it was over the North African desert. More Blenheim squadrons – Nos. 34, 42 and 113 – and No. 5 Squadron, which had been flying the Mohawk since December 1941, also re-equipped with the potent Hurricane Mk IID and the Mk IIC. The Hurricane was going from strength to strength in the Far East, especially as the Indian Air Force (IAF) began re-equipping eight of its squadrons with the type, of which more than 300 were delivered before the end of the war. The IAF Hurricanes flew side-by-side with their RAF counterparts during the Arakan and Imphal campaigns.

The Sea Hurricane had also persisted in the Far East, serving on Pacific convoy escort duties aboard HMS *Nairana* and *Vindex* into 1944. But from February the Hurricane's importance in the Far East began to decline. The beginning of the end was marked by No. 67 Squadron, which relinquished its Hurricane Mk IICs for the Spitfire Mk VIII, while No. 17 Squadron did the same in May. Also in May, No. 135 Squadron, which had been flying the Hurricane since August 1941, became the first RAF unit to receive the US-built Republic Thunderbolt; Nos. 79, 146 and 261 Squadrons re-equipped in June, No. 30 Squadron in July, Nos. 134 and 258 Squadrons in September and No. 5 Squadron in October 1944.

Number 20 Squadron had used the Hurricane Mk IID with distinction during the second Arakan campaign and later, along with No. 60 Squadron, received the Mk IV. But re-equipping with the Thunderbolt and Spitfire continued through early 1945, and by the war's end only No. 20 Squadron and the IAF units still flew the Hurricane operationally in the Far East.

It is only in recent years that the Hurricane's contribution to the outcome of World War II has been fully appreciated. The Spitfire was on a pedestal from the beginning, strongly emphasised in the September 1945 Battle of Britain flypast, led by Group Captain Douglas Bader DSO DFC, a survivor of the Battle of Britain and ex-Hurricane pilot, flying a Spitfire. Not a single Hurricane was on display,

LEFT A student Indian Air Force pilot with flying kit photographed beside his Hurricane before a training flight at Kohat, in the North West Frontier Province of India, circa 1943. (Photo by Cecil Beaton/IWM via Getty Images)

a mere five years after the end of one of the world's most crucial aerial battles. Post-war Britain was not a place for sentimentality, and even Sydney Camm was in no mood to dwell on the past as he forged ahead with jet designs for the future, high-tech RAF.

However, those who had flown the Hurricane, whether in the skies over south-east England, the North African deserts or the jungles of the Far East, retained fond memories of the aircraft. Bader himself was pleasantly surprised when he first flew the Hurricane in June 1940, describing what seemed like a big aircraft on the ground as being, when airborne, highly manoeuvrable, harmonised, viceless, strong and a superb gun platform, remaining 'rock-steady' when all eight guns were fired.

Its ability to out-turn a Spitfire and, more significantly, a Bf 109, cancelled out the fact that it was 30mph slower than the enemy fighter. This difference in performance was reduced with later marks, but by this time the Hurricane was becoming a dedicated ground aircraft, a role in which it would see more action than any other.

In a nutshell, the Hurricane operated and fought in considerably more campaigns, on more fronts, and in more theatres and countries than any other aircraft during World War II. Only the Blenheim came close to matching it, while the 'big' names of the conflict fell far behind. On top of that, the Hurricane shot down more enemy aircraft than any other RAF aircraft during the war.

OPPOSITE Hurricanes flying in formation during the Battle of Britain. (Photo by Universal History Archive/Getty Images)

HURRICANE ACES

Many pilots reached ace status by scoring five or more air-to-air victories over enemy aircraft on the Hurricane. Their stories are legion, but since space precludes doing justice to even a few of them, it perhaps makes sense to examine the experiences of Edgar James 'Cobber' Kain, the first RAF Hurricane ace, and the exploits of its most successful, Marmaduke Thomas St John 'Pat' Pattle and his comrades, over Greece.

'COBBER' KAIN – FIRST HURRICANE ACE

The last of the three Hurricanes gently bumped down on the grass strip at Rouvres, its pilot throttling back

OPPOSITE On 8 November 1939, Flying Officer E. J. 'Cobber' Kain, in his Hurricane Mk I 'P' Paddy III, spotted and fired on a lone Dornier Do 17P being flown over Metz. Although the bomber tried to escape into cloud, Kain climbed and opened fire from 250 yards, sending the Dornier into an inescapable vertical dive. The stricken plane hit the ground at 500mph and exploded on impact, giving Kain his first kill. (Simon Smith © Osprey Publishing)

and rolling out in the direction of his dispersal. Watching from their cockpits, a further trio of No. 73 Squadron pilots continued their preparations for the next patrol over the Franco-German border.

Word quickly filtered through to them that the returned section had engaged the enemy, with some success. This hastened the heartbeat and moistened the palms of two of the pilots, who were yet to encounter the Luftwaffe. Fortunately for them, however, their section leader had already left his mark on the enemy, destroying two Do 17 bombers and a single Bf 109E in previous skirmishes. Despite being their junior in age, Flying Officer Edgar James 'Cobber' Kain was the squadron's best and most combat-experienced pilot.

Keen to see if more German aircraft were aloft in the vicinity of the Saar River (barely 30 miles from Rouvres), New Zealander Kain signalled to his groundcrew to switch on the starter trolley connected to his aircraft (possibly L1766). With electricity pouring into the power unit, Kain flicked on the main magneto switches and the starter magneto and the Merlin II turned over, the propeller spun and the engine fired into action. Within a minute, all three fighters had barked into life. After a quick confirmation by the section leader that his two pilots were happy with their aircraft, Kain waved the starter trolleys and wheel chocks away and led his charges out from the dispersal.

Take-off was completed with little fuss, 'B' Flight's Green Section closed up into the standard RAF fighter 'vic' formation and then climbed in an easterly direction towards the German border town of Saarbrücken. Their patrol height on this Tuesday afternoon was to be 20,000ft and the formation levelled off at this altitude barely eight minutes after departing Rouvres.

Kain knew exactly where the German border was, having already gained a reputation among RAF fighter pilots within the AASF for patrolling deep into enemy territory, as fellow AASF pilot and future Hurricane ace, Paul Richey, attested: '"Cobber" Kain was 73's most split-arse pilot. He often led a section 40 miles or more into Germany, regardless of the fact that it was against orders to cross the frontier.'

On this occasion, Green Section had barely crossed the 'Siegfried Line' when Kain spotted nine III./JG 53 'Pik As' Bf 109Es cruising in a wide vic at 26,000ft. Despite being outnumbered, the Kiwi pilot skilfully manoeuvred his flight into an advantageous position then made his move. Initially only two enemy fighters responded to the attack, Kain's gunsight quickly filling with the grey-green shape of the leading 'Emil'. He pressed the gun button on his spade-grip control column at a range of less than 250 yards, and the Hurricane shuddered as all eight .303in Brownings spewed forth a deadly hail of bullets. The tracer rounds arced across the sky and hit their target with telling effect.

The Bf 109E fell away trailing smoke and flame, and Kain wheeled around in search of further targets.

OPPOSITE Flying Officers N. 'Fanny' Orton and E. J. 'Cobber' Kain of No. 73 Squadron standing by a Hawker Hurricane Mk I, between sorties, at Reims-Champagne. Orton left France with at least 15 victories and Kain with 17. (© IWM C 1564)

Following their leader into the fray, Flying Officer J. C. 'Tub' Perry (who was killed in a landing accident just three days later) and Sergeant T. B. G. 'Titch' Pyne (lost on 14 May 1940, one of three No. 73 Squadron pilots killed in combat with Bf 109Es that day) had also chosen targets on this opening pass as more enemy fighters committed to the engagement. Both pilots quickly expended all their ammunition in the excitement of their first combat, Perry later being credited with a Bf 109E destroyed, while Pyne's claim was rated as only a probable.

A second 'Pik As' Schwarm (comprising four aircraft) of Emils then entered the fray from a higher altitude, much to Kain's consternation – he had thought the battle was over. As the only pilot left with any ammunition in his magazines, Kain immediately latched onto one of the overshooting Bf 109Es and fired a burst into it. Having been surprised by the second enemy formation, he had not been best placed from a tactical standpoint when it came to engaging these 'latecomers'. As Kain attempted to manoeuvre 'up sun' of the fleeing Messerschmitts, a well-aimed burst of cannon fire blew his Hurricane's canopy clean off.

Feldwebel Weigelt had been flying towards the rear of the second Schwarm, and had shadowed the solitary Hurricane as its pilot attempted to achieve a better angle of deflection on the Bf 109Es ahead of him. He pumped further rounds into Kain's mortally wounded fighter, which erupted in flames when tracer ignited spilt fuel from the punctured reserve, or gravity tank ahead of the cockpit. The German pilot could see his RAF counterpart hunched down in the now exposed cockpit, which was all but engulfed by the conflagration. Dazed, Kain fumbled around blindly to his left in an attempt to shut off the fuel cock, and thus hopefully stop the fire.

At this point Weigelt hit the Hurricane with a third burst, which drove no less than 21 shell splinters into Kain's left calf. Realising he was fighting a lost cause and in some pain from both shrapnel wounds and burns to his right hand, the Kiwi pilot gingerly undid his straps, rolled his blazing Hurricane onto its back

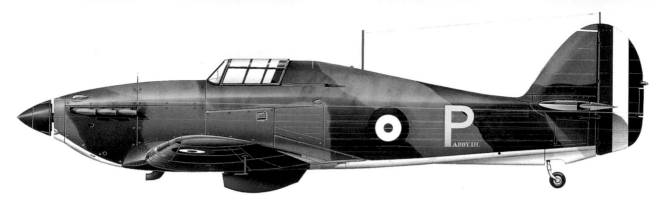

Hurricane Mk I of No. 73 Squadron, flown by Flying Officer E. J. Kain, Rouvres, France, early spring 1940. The exact identity of this aircraft remains a mystery, as all No. 73 Squadron 'Phoney War' Hurricane Is had had their serials obliterated by the spring of 1940 for security reasons. (Keith Fretwell © Osprey Publishing)

and fell away from the stricken machine. He quickly pulled the ripcord of his parachute upon entering a cloud, before passing out from physical exhaustion. Kain came to minutes later in cloud, and landed in a field near the small French border village of Ritzing, just half a mile west of Germany.

His two colleagues returned to Rouvres unscathed and quickly reported their engagement to No. 73 Squadron's adjutant, Pilot Officer 'Henry' Hall. A search party was sent out to retrieve 'Cobber' Kain and he was soon located and conveyed back to his unit in a French army staff car. The wounded pilot was debriefed from his bed, and his two claims for Bf 109Es destroyed officially recorded – post-war Luftwaffe records for 26 March 1940 note the force-landing of three Bf 109Es at Trier airfield in the aftermath of this action.

As the first RAF ace of World War II, the tall, rangy, 21-year-old New Zealander celebrated 'acedom' that evening in true air force fashion – horizontally, on a stretcher in the sergeant's mess!

'PAT' PATTLE – HURRICANE ACE OF ACES

On 28 October 1940, Italian forces invaded Greece and among the RAF units despatched in response was the experienced Gladiator-equipped No. 80 Squadron. It would soon make its mark. In mid-February 1941, the squadron received Hurricanes for operations at Paramythia, near the Albanian border. At the same time, No. 33 Squadron's Hurricanes moved to Greece from North Africa, the unit numbering among its ranks several successful pilots including Flying Officers Charles Dyson (nine victories), Vernon Woodward (eight), Frank Holman (one), Peter Wickham (four) and John Mackie (six), and Flight Sergeant Len Cottingham (six).

Number 80 Squadron flew the first Hurricane operation in Greece on the 20th, led by the unit's top-scoring pilot, Flight Lieutenant 'Pat' Pattle. On the way back to base, Pattle spotted some Italian fighters, as his biography relates:

> He led his section straight towards four Fiat G.50s and, shouting to Sergeant Casbolt and 'Timber' Woods to attack individually, selected the leading G.50 as his own target. As he approached, the dark green Fiat pulled away into a steep turn, but Pat managed to hold it in his sights until he came into range and thumbed the gun button. It was the first time he had fired the eight guns of the Hurricane, and the result was astonishing. The G.50 exploded right before his eyes, disintegrating into hundreds of small flaming pieces.

The Hurricane had shot down its first victim over Greece. Casbolt claimed two, and after landing, so did Woods. It was a highly successful debut that ensured

OPPOSITE Squadron Leader Marmaduke Thomas St John 'Pat' Pattle, Officer Commanding No. 33 Squadron, and the Squadron Adjutant, Flight Lieutenant George Rumsey, standing by a Hurricane at Larissa, Thessaly, Greece. (© IWM ME(RAF) 1260)

ascendancy was maintained. Pattle's Fiat was from 154° Gruppo, and the first of around 35 victories that the South African would claim while flying the Hurricane over the next two months.

Number 33's detachment began operations alongside No. 80 Squadron on 27 February when it intercepted Italian bombers (escorted by CR.42s) over Valona. The unit's Sergeant Ted Hewett claimed two to take his total to five, while No. 33's Sergeant Len Cottingham scored his outfit's first Hurricane victory, which also made him an ace, and Flying Officer Harry Starrett shared another.

The next afternoon there was a huge dogfight between RAF and Italian fighters over the frontline. The Italians were routed, although British claims for 27 destroyed were certainly inflated. Pattle, in V7589, destroyed two fighters and two 37° Stormo Fiat BR.20 bombers. Flying Officer Richard Acworth (detached from No. 112 Squadron) sent down a BR.20 for his fifth. Flying Officer 'Ape' Cullen (who had flown V7138) wrote of his first Hurricane combat:

The battle extended right across Albania. First, I found four Breda 20s [*sic*]. I got one, which went down in flames. Then we found three formations of SM.79s. I took on one and aimed at the starboard engine. It caught fire and crashed in flames. I climbed and dived on the next. He too crashed in flames. Then we attacked ten CR.42s, climbing to get above them. I got behind one, and he caught fire and went down in flames. Up again immediately – dived, fired into the cockpit and another took fire, rolled over and crashed. I had to come home then – no more ammo.

After this extraordinary combat, the young Australian received an immediate DFC. Meanwhile, Pattle had landed and then returned to the fray in another aircraft and shot down two more CR.42s. It was the RAF's most successful day of the campaign.

During the morning of 3 March Cullen, Acworth and Pilot Officer Bill Vale intercepted a mixed formation of CANT Z.1007 and SM.81 bombers heading for Larissa. Acworth shot down a CANT,

Cullen claimed four more and Vale scored his first Hurricane kill (his 14th victory), recording tersely in his log book, '1025, interception Patrol (one S.81)'.

The next day, both squadrons escorted a force attacking Italian warships. As they neared Valona six G.50s dived on them, Pattle sending one into a mountainside north of Himare. However, a second Fiat jumped Cullen, and the 15-victory Australian ace crashed and was killed. Pattle continued, shooting down two more G.50s, while Sergeant Hewett was busy claiming a G.50 and three CR.42s. Bill Vale also shot down a G.50.

Pattle left No. 80 Squadron shortly afterwards to take command of No. 33 Squadron. He was regarded with the utmost respect by his peers, one of whom, Squadron Leader (later Air Marshal Sir) Paddy Dunn said of him: 'Air fighting was his game. Pattle was a remarkable man, with an easy and natural manner. In Greece his courage and indomitable leadership became legendary – an exceptional fighter leader and a brilliant pilot.'

On 23 March, Squadron Leader Pattle led an attack against Fier airfield, where No. 33 Squadron was jumped by 20 G.50s. One fell to 'Woody' Woodward, another to Pattle and a third to Flying Officer Frank Holman. At around this time, during a lull in the fighting, No. 80 Squadron at last became fully re-equipped with Hurricanes. There were some Italian attacks during this period, such as on 2 April when a group of Z.1007s lost three of their number to 'Woody' Woodward. He shot two down in flames on his first diving pass before attacking a third, which ditched in the Gulf of Patras.

BLITZKRIEG

On 6 April the Germans invaded the Balkans, and at a stroke transformed the British situation in Greece. The RAF was soon in action and, as ever, Pattle was to the fore when No. 33 Squadron mounted an offensive patrol over Bulgaria. There he claimed his first German victims – 8./JG 27 Bf 109Es. Oberleutnant Arno Becker was killed and Leutnant Klaus Faber captured. Len Cottingham shot down a third Bf 109 and another fell to Flying Officer Peter Wickham, his first success in the Hurricane. However, the Greek collapse in eastern Macedonia allowed a rapid German move southwards, forcing a British withdrawal.

During the afternoon of 12 April, Pattle led a sweep up the rugged Struma valley, where No. 33 Squadron encountered a lone Dornier, which he shot down. Then directed to Larissa, his formation found three escorted SM.79s. Ordering some of his force to attack the fighters, Pattle led Harry Starrett and Frankie Holman down on the bombers, claiming one while the other two shared a second.

Number 80 Squadron was also heavily engaged. During a bomber escort over Bulgaria on the 14th, Vale, in V7795, shot down a Ju 87, recording the event in his logbook: '1250 – Bomber escort over Bulgaria (one Ju 87)'. This aircraft was probably the most successful individual Hurricane of the Greek campaign; it was delivered to No. 80 Squadron as a reinforcement on 9 April and Bill Vale flew it regularly over the next six weeks.

The Germans had begun heavy attacks on RAF airfields, and at Larissa on the 15th a future ace had a narrow escape. One of the groundcrew, Aircraftsman 2 D. F. Harris described it vividly:

I dashed out of our ridge tent to see a sight I'll never forget as three very brave pilots stood their Hurricanes on their tails to gain height – 15 yellow-nosed Messerschmitt 109s were coming at them out of the dawn sun. The first to go was Pilot Officer Chatham when his aircraft was cut in half by enemy fire. Flight Lieutenant Jackie stalled in on one wing, his guns firing to the last. Sergeant Genders gained some height and managed to survive to land later on. One of the '109s was shot down and the pilot baled out.

Harris saw Jackie's victim fall. In his first combat, George Genders had brought down Feldwebel Kohler of 4./JG 77 and within a week, the 21-year old was credited with four more victories.

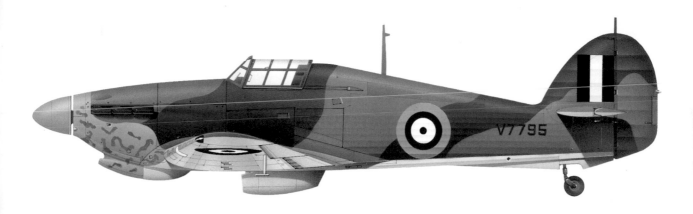

Hurricane I V7795 of Pilot Officer W. Vale, No 80 Squadron. Possibly the most successful Hurricane of the Greek campaign, V7795 was extensively used by Bill Vale. There was no time to apply unit markings, and it flew as depicted. (John Weal © Osprey Publishing)

Another claiming his first victory that day was Pilot Officer Roald Dahl, who shot down a Ju 88, while Vale went one better by downing two Junkers bombers over Athens in V7795, getting another on the 16th and two Stukas over Larissa on the 18th.

DEATH OVER PIRAEUS

On 19 April – a day of continuous raids – Woodward shared Henschel Hs 126 '6K+AH' of 1(H)./23 with Pattle and another pilot. He recalled, 'Pattle was mad. He had gone down to attack the Hs 126 and the rest of the flight followed to join in the fun.

No one thought to provide top cover.' Leaving the area, they met nine Bf 109s, but Pattle and Woodward pulled into Zimmerman turns that put them onto the tails of the enemy fighters, with the result that Squadron Leader Pattle shot down two and Woodward one.

By now both Hurricane squadrons were greatly reduced in strength, and concentrated at Eleusis, near Athens. There they faced a sustained Luftwaffe assault. During an early patrol on the 20th, Frankie Holman belly-landed on marshy ground, but the aircraft overturned and the pilot broke his neck, killing him instantly.

Worse was to follow that afternoon when a huge raid of more than 100 bombers, with fighter escort, was reported heading for the harbour at Piraeus to attack shipping. The last surviving Hurricanes – nine from No. 33 and six from No. 80 Squadron – were scrambled. Among the first to arrive over the port were Peter Wickham, Harry Starrett and Flying Officer 'Ping' Newton. They followed some Ju 88s into their dives, Newton shooting down two for his first victories.

Wickham got another, while Bill Vale, who arrived to claim two, recalled, 'One caught fire and started going down so I left him and attacked another. Big chunks broke away from his wings and fuselage and smoke poured from his engines. He went down vertically.' Starrett, in V7804, was hit and his Hurricane caught fire. In an attempt to save the aircraft he headed for Eleusis, but as he touched down the fighter was enveloped in flames and he later succumbed to his injuries.

Other Hurricanes from No. 80 Squadron were by now engaging a mass of Do 17s and Bf 110s. Sergeant Casbolt claimed two, then, as he pulled away, a Bf 109 crossed his path and he sent that down in flames too. Sergeant Ted Hewett attacked six Bf 109s, reporting, 'I dived on the rear one and he rolled on his back and crashed to the ground with smoke pouring out. I made a similar attack on a second and the pilot baled out.' These victories took his total to 16. Some pilots had returned to Eleusis, and having replenished their fuel and ammunition, headed back to the fight, led by a very ill Pattle on his third sortie of the day. Vernon Woodward later recalled:

I took off late with Sqn Ldr Pattle. We climbed into a swarm of Ju 88s protected by masses of Messerschmitt 110s. We were overwhelmed. In sun, I recall shooting a '110 off Pattle's tail, in flames, then probably a Ju 88. Shortly afterwards Pattle got a confirmed '110. Subsequently, I lost contact with him.

Ahead of him, Woodward had witnessed his CO attempting to aid his friend, 'Timber' Woods, who was being attacked by a Bf 110. He had seen its demise just as Woods' aircraft burst into flames and crashed into the bay. Two other Bf 110s then swept onto Pattle's Hurricane, which caught fire and exploded. It too crashed into Eleusis Bay, taking with it the RAF's most successful fighter pilot. Flight Lieutenant Jimmie Kettlewell witnessed Pattle's end, before attacking and shooting down one of the Bf 110s to score his fifth victory. Then he too was hit and forced to bail out, injuring his back on landing. Another of No. 33 Squadron's aces, Flight Sergeant Len Cottingham, also bailed out wounded, but not before he had downed three Bf 110s. It had been a truly disastrous afternoon for the RAF fighters.